God the future of man

God the Future of Man

Edward Schillebeeckx

Translated N. D. Smith

074146

Sheed and Ward
London

Contents

Introduction

During my lecture tour in the United States (from November 8th to December 20th, 1967), I was repeatedly asked whether the lecture that I was giving would be published, so that it would later be read at leisure. This gave me the idea of collecting all the lectures given during the tour and publishing them: this, then, is the reason for the appearance of this volume.

The book begins with the five lectures prepared for the tour. As a matter of fact, I often gave quite different lectures under the same headings—the titles had been announced in advance by the organizing authorities, but in very general terms. It happened that in response to the questions and ideas of various audiences, one entirely new lecture emerged, and this was the starting-point from which developed what is offered here as Chapter VI. But the main body of the book consists of the unchanged text of the five lectures which I prepared before the tour commenced and in the form in which I gave them during the first stage of the tour.

But (as I have said elsewhere) giving lectures is not only "giving." The discussion period, and above all the personal conversations that follow the lectures, mean also a "receiving," and frequently these are not simply informative answers but also questions which force one to reflect—to rethink the problem. Apart from the lecture on the "new hermeneutics," the theme of all the lectures was to a great extent that of religion and secularization, viewed from various vantage-points—secularization and speaking of God, secularization and the problem of the Church's liturgy, secularization and the Church's new understanding of herself arising from this (the Church as dialogue) and, finally, secularization and the future of mankind on earth seen in the light of the *eschaton* (the Church and social politics).

It was precisely this problem—Christian secularity—that was the theme of the Notre Dame symposium, in which, for three days (from the 17th until the 19th of November, 1967), twenty-seven theologians of many different confessions studied the problem of "death of God" theology. But it was not in the first place this symposium—they seemed to accept my contribution on "secularization and speaking and silence about God" gladly and without criticism (see Chapter 2 of this book)—but rather the questions asked during the discussion period after my lectures and in my personal conversations with theologians and sociologists which led me to reflect again about the real meaning of "secularization."

For this reason, I conclude this book with a new article (first published in the Dutch *Tijdschrift voor Theologie,* pt. 8, 1968, pp. 44–66) in which I consider anew, in the light of my experiences in the United States, the problem with which I had been dealing there. This subsequent reflection led me to make certain modifications in connection with the phenomenon of "secularization" which, in turn, led to my outlining a concept of God which can function meaningfully in our new culture which honors the primacy of the future—"God as man's future."

The publication of this book may also be evidence of the

debt of gratitude which I owe to Sheed and Ward of New York who have organized the publication of the material of such a complicated lecture tour so efficiently, to my translator, N. D. Smith, who time and again willingly worked over-time, to my assistant, T. M. Schoof, O.P., who gave me expert help with, among other things, the difficulties of English pro-nunciation and to my Flemish compatriot, A. Truyman, O.P., who accompanied me during my American tour as travelling companion and secretary and performed unforgettable services for me in the United States. Finally, I must not forget my brother in religion, lay-brother Tharsicius Wilbrink, O.P., who has devotedly deciphered my handwriting and retyped my work. It is to all these silent helpers that this book is gratefully dedicated.

Nijmegen, the Netherlands   E. Schillebeeckx, o.p.
19 February 1968

I

Towards a Catholic Use of Hermeneutics

"The situation could hardly be more grotesque—my philosophical attempts are proclaimed as the destruction of metaphysics and yet, at the same time, with the help of these attempts, ways of thought and ideas are followed which have been derived from—I do not say which are indebted to—that alleged destruction."
—Martin Heidegger, *Zur Seinsfrage*[1]

The new hermeneutics has arisen from the quest for a method
of proclaiming the evangelical message which will bring it
home to twentieth-century man: a proclamation which will on
the one hand remain faithful to the word of God and on the
other hand will allow that word to ring out in a way which
does not by-pass the reality of his life. Everyone since Bultmann who has taken the hermeneutical problem seriously is in
agreement with this intention, but there is considerable diver-
gence of opinion as to the paths which should be followed if
a contemporary proclamation of the true Christian message is
to be attained. The issue which is central here is that of the involvement of theology with reality. Is the claim that faith and
theology have a bearing on the reality of our lives legitimate? Or
does not theology in fact draw us away from the vital realities
of our existence, leading us into a strange realm which only
borders on the real world? Is the "newer" theology, with its
pronounced stress on hermeneutics, not a reaction against what
might be described as the "schizophrenic" approach of the
"older" theology to the realities of our human condition?

Whichever path has been followed since Bultmann, that of
"existential" theology[2] or that of the theology which takes
"revelation as history"[3] as its point of departure—these two
being the "new" paths competing, at the moment, for pride

of place—one thing is in any case clear: the basic trend requires that faith shall involve an understanding of our own concrete lives and that the sphere in which the intelligibility of God and our way of speaking of God manifest themselves shall be set forth within this understanding. In the attempt to bring this about the "newer" theology is, all appearances to the contrary, the opposite of liberal theology—which Bultmann himself wished to abandon. The "new hermeneutics" seeks to expose the ontological structures of the theological understanding of reality as a totality. It is an attempt to clarify the presuppositions of the theological quest for reality in a situation wherein man, estranged from history and nature, raises the question of the meaninglessness of a world which he himself has created by technical and scientific ingenuity and is inclined to regard as the only relevant reality.

We may not agree with the final solutions for this problem which existential theology and the theology of history have tried to provide and may even find them regrettable. Nevertheless we must all admit that these theologians are all concerned with saving the *Christian* faith from the process of "loss of reality" which is taking place in our technical world.[4] We may question whether the Christian faith is emerging intact from this reinterpretation, but we certainly cannot deny that the whole intention of this theology is to help the faith to pass unscathed through its present-day crisis, whereas the "older" theology is simply repeating itself and rendering no assistance to the faith in this time of trial. Thus the older theology is at least equally endangering orthodoxy, if only because, in remaining so ill-adapted to modern needs, it is increasing the numbers of those who fall away from the faith—both those who noisily protest and those who leave quietly.

In this chapter, I shall both formulate the problem as clearly as possible and analyze and criticize the new solutions, in order to open up, via hermeneutics of history, a perspective within which, in my opinion, faithfulness to the biblical message *in* the reinterpretation of faith will continue to be guaranteed.

THE HERMENEUTICAL PROBLEM

The "Hermeneutical Circle"

1. *The New Question.* It has long been clear that we are not addressed by a *nuda vox Dei,* a word from God without alloy coming down to us, as it were, vertically in a purely divine statement. God's word is given to us within the already inter-pretative response to it of the Old and New Testaments—believers who had found the ground of their being in God's faithfulness bore witness interpretatively to God's saving actions in Israel and in the man Jesus, the Christ, the foundation of their hope for a renewed world, and their witness was interpreted in its turn. The God of salvation was made the subject of a *conversation between men*—it was in this way that God's word was addressed to us. This human dialogue in which God gave himself to be understood was as such necessarily *situated* —it had a social setting, a living historical context. It is even possible to distinguish in the Old and New Testaments, within the development of the final text, various successive "new contexts" in which an earlier dialogue has been reinterpreted in the light of a new situation, but in such a way that the content of the earlier dialogue is seen as *authoritative* in this new interpretation. Even outside its original context, this earlier dialogue apparently retained its vitality and relevance for believers in their changing situations. In this way we have not only God's words as they were first understood: the content of his mes-

sage reaches us in a context enriched by the meditation on the
faith of the early Christians, constantly listening and interpreting the words for themselves in their own hearts. It is the
spirit of God who is at work in the words addressed to men
and in the interpretative listening to this message; the Spirit
who, within the ecclesial sphere of early Christianity, keeps us
mindful of the Event and its meaning. Holy Scripture is, as it
were, the canonical archives against which the unceasing remembrance of the Church (always calling to mind the word
of God in the midst of changing circumstances) can be veri-
fied by the whole people of God, guided and accompanied by
the "apostolic office" of the Church.

A serious tension is inherent in this situation. A message of
God to men expressed and interpreted in a specific historical
situation of the past becomes the norm for, and the test of, *our*
Christian faith today—a faith that is experienced in a totally
different historical situation. The essential implication of this
is that we can comprehend this biblical word in faith only
through a reinterpretative understanding of the faith and in
no other way. We cannot grasp the biblical text directly "in
itself," as though we, as readers or believers, *transcended time*.

This "thesis" is commonly held to have originated with Bultmann and the theologians who have followed him, but in
reality, though Catholics seldom appear to be aware of the fact,
it is one of the essential elements of Catholic theology. However, it has been presented thematically not in terms of "hermeneutics" but in terms of the "development of dogma,"
which is the Catholic counterpart of what is known in Protestant theology as the "hermeneutical" problem. The Catholic
sense of dogma—for example, the christological dogma of
Chalcedon—implies, after all, that the biblical view of Christ
has been reinterpreted in the light of the Church's experience

and the secular and social situation in the fifth century and, what is more, in such a way that this new interpretation really expresses precisely the *same* datum of faith that is promised to us in the Bible and no other—the same datum *in* a reinterpretative testimony. What else does this mean but that the fifth-century situation enters essentially into the statement of faith itself, without the real content of faith becoming *different?* The *same* thing is said in a *different* way, since dogma is a point of faith—that is, not a theological statement but a declaration of the biblical datum by the Church. Dogma, after all, is an assent *in faith* on the part of the universal Church. Essentially, the road that led from the Bible to Chalcedon is no different from that which led, for example, from the original image of Christ to that of the synoptics and Paul and later to that of John. The hermeneutical problem is therefore given a full-length portrait in this: the contemporary scene with its understanding of its own existence is a "hermeneutical" situation, and it is only within this and from this situation (certainly not outside it or from above) that we can understand in faith what the biblical message itself gives us to understand.

This Catholic interpretation of the "development of dogma" implies in a specific way what, on the basis of Heidegger especially,[5] both Bultmann and his followers[6] and, independently of this school, Protestant philosophers such as P. Ricoeur[7] and H.-G. Gadamer[8] and Protestant theologians such as Paul Tillich and K. Löwith[9] have called the "hermeneutical circle." All understanding takes place in a circular movement—the answer is to some extent determined by the question, which is in turn confirmed, extended or corrected by the answer. A new question then grows out of this understanding, so that the hermeneutical circle continues to develop in a never-ending spiral. Man can never escape from this circle, because he can never establish once and for all the truth or the content of the word of God. There is no definitive, timeless understanding which raises no more questions. The "hermeneutical circle" thus has its basis in the historicity of human existence and therefore of all human understanding. The interpreter belongs to some extent to the object itself that he is trying to understand, that is, the historical phenomenon. All understanding is therefore a form of self-understanding.

In our understanding in faith of the text of the Bible, our own existence, which has grown out of the past and is in the present directed towards the future, plays a hermeneutical role. It is precisely in the light of our own new and different situation that we ask the Bible questions and expect the Bible itself to answer these questions. Our understanding of a text takes place in a circular movement—in every interpretation, our obligation to tradition (the text) and the corresponding possibilities for the future both play a part. The content of the biblical text acts as a norm for our interpretation, but the text can only give an intelligible answer within the new sphere of questioning, which makes it possible to look *beyond* what is explicitly said in the text. The answer to this contemporary question can, however, never be the literal repetition of a biblical or conciliar text. In that case, the text that we are seeking to understand would not be an *answer*. It is only within our own sphere of questioning, derived from our living relationship with the same reality which is directly or indirectly expressed in the Bible (that is, human existence, together with man's understanding of himself that is given in this existence—at least in the restricted phenomenological sense given to it by Bultmann) that Scripture can provide an answer that is intelligible to us, because it is only in this way that Scripture does answer our real problems. Thus the meaning of a text is indeed related to the question that is asked— it is only in the context of this question that the text can be meaningfully understood. The answer (which is nonetheless given by the *text* itself) thus transcends what is literally in the text. And yet the interpreter is obedient to the authority of the text and his asking of questions and his preliminary drafting of answers are constantly corrected in a contemporary reinterpretative understanding of the text itself. In the case of Bultmann, the hermeneutical circle ultimately develops into a circle between self-understanding (man's understanding of his own existence) and the understanding of faith, from which the whole of his "existentialistic interpretation" of the New Testament follows.

Contrary to what has often been asserted, Bultmann did not in any way intend his "existentialistic interpretation" of the Bible (the interpretation of the Bible from an "existential" sphere of questioning, that is from questions which concern our existence) to be a dogmatic presupposition which would determine what is essentially inviolable and what is changeable in faith. He was positive in his denial of this[10] (although his narrow concept of existence can in fact be called a strong presupposition). According to Bultmann, existentialistic interpretation has a purely hermeneutical character—how must the Bible be understood? What are the questions susceptible to biblical inquiry, the questions to which consequently a meaningful biblical answer can be expected? These are, in Bultmann's view, questions about human existential potentialities—the question of self-understanding. The questions which he asks the Bible are perhaps—and, in my opinion, certainly in some cases—asked on a basis which is understood too narrowly and limited too much to existentialistic preoccupations.

There is, in other words, more to be understood in the Bible than he regards as "intelligible" in it. But we, for our part, should not forget that these things which are beyond the scope of such an inquiry must also be *understood;* otherwise faith might become, to put it crudely, no more than a matter of regarding as true a number of affirmations which in fact contradict the legitimacy of present-day scientific thought and our contemporary view of man and the world.

The difficulty, however, is that most of the authors who appeal to the "hermeneutical circle" within which human existence is acted out seem to have placed the problem of *truth* on a slippery slope. They rightly stress the historicity of truth, but there is no sign of any attempt on their part to show how truth, in this historicity, is more than a historical expression that changes in each period—that is, how it is *truth* and not simply "authenticity," something that may be appealing to man in constantly new situations. We may indeed wonder whether Bultmannism does not suffer most grievously from what Heidegger, the most perceptive diagnostician of Western European thought, has called "forgetfulness of being," a blind spot in man's thinking which causes him to lapse one-sidedly, not into objectivism in this case, but into pure existentiality.

2. *The Older Solution: The Kernel and Its Mode of Expression.* In the whole of this problem, the "changeableness" and the "unchangeableness," or indefectibility, of the Christian message, the Christian confession and the Christian dogma are all at stake. Expressed in this way, as a distinguishing of what is changeable and what is unchangeable, the problem does indeed seem to be insoluble, but it is then falsely posed. It is most profoundly a question of the identity of faith *in* the re-integration itself of faith and not a question of an "unchange-

able element of faith," as though this could ever be isolated. The christology of the Bible (the biblical *interpretation* of Jesus of Nazareth) and the christology of Chalcedon (the interpretation in faith of the biblical interpretation and thus a reinterpretation) clearly bear witness to two different social contexts and worlds of thought, yet they also bear witness at the same time to the one, imperishable faith in Jesus, the Christ, our Lord. We live, in 1968, in a very different period. What does the word say to *us* in the Bible? It says the same thing, but it says it in a contemporary interpretation.

A traditional distinction has always been made between the "essential dogmatic affirmation" (the *id quod*) and its "mode of expression" (the *modus cum quo*). The first pointed to the "unchangeable essence," the second to the changeable, varying elements. I too have already made use of this distinction, but only either implicitly[11] or explicitly[12] in a retrospective sense. Retrospectively, this distinction is precise and meaningful, but it fails us at the exact moment that we really need it—in a contemporary interpretation of authentic faith. This distinction is, in other words, only meaningful when it has no longer any significance for us existentially. We can make this distinction in an earlier interpretation once a new interpretation has already been provided and also accepted by the whole community of believers—we can, for example, understand the Aristotelian "twin" term substance-accident as a mode of expression when we look back at the Tridentine theologians' views of transubstantiation. In truth, this only means that those theologians were genuinely able to *understand* the real datum of faith in that interpretation, that it was capable of being grasped by them in those terms. If we then discard that mode in which the reality was worded, we are left with a content; it is, however, no more the "pure content of faith" than the earlier one was, but is simply a faithful *interpretation* in the light of our present situation. This interpretation, not a "timeless essence," contains for us the "pure content of faith."

The problem only becomes difficult, then, when the Church is in a period of transition between an earlier interpretation and a new one and there is still no certainty as to whether the attempted reinterpretation of a datum of faith is in fact a real understanding *of faith*. In our present-day understanding of transubstantiation, of the figure of Christ, of the unique sonship of Christ in relation to the traditional datum of the "virgin birth" and so on, what is the real essence and what is *our* mode of expressing this essential element? We know *a priori* that there is a distinction here, because the social and historical element can never be eliminated from our thought and our understanding of faith. The difference between the "dogmatic essence" and its historical "mode of expression" is therefore an unassailable datum, but it is also virtually meaningless and unmanageable, precisely because this "essence" is never given to us as a pure essence, but is always concealed *in* a historical mode of expression. A partial affirmation *is,* after all, never completely true. No distinction can therefore be made in it between a completely true, unchangeable essence and changeable modes of expressing this essence—the absolute penetrates all relative interpretations, the one is never present without the other. Believing always comes about as interpretative understanding. The interpretative aspect is contained in a noetic perspective of faith that can never, in itself, be thematized or conceptualized, an orientation towards the saving reality, determined by that reality, which finds expression in the interpretation of faith. What is known as the "essence" or kernel can only be reached via and in historically profiled approaches, just as one points with one's finger in one particular

direction, and not in any other, because it is in that direction
that the reality which one intends, but cannot define any more
precisely, is situated.

Existentially, this traditional distinction means nothing
more than this—but this is in itself extremely valuable—that
our own contemporary interpretations are also inadequate
attempts to suggest the mystery in a meaningful and objective
way and at the same time to make it capable of being experienced in these interpretations. We know beforehand that they
themselves will become outdated. The demythologization
that we apply to the biblical story will later on have to be applied, and correctly, to our own twentieth-century story, because the story continues. The question is, then, What is it that
gives continuity and therefore intelligibility to the whole of
this story?

3. *"What is Said" and "What is Intended."* The distinction
between the "essential dogmatic affirmation" and its "mode of
expression" recurs in a rather different perspective in Bultmann as the distinction between "what is said" (*das Gesagte*)
and "what is intended" (*das Gemeinte*).[13] What is said must
be measured against and interpreted in the light of what is
intended, the matter with which the interpreter is concerned
and with which he, directly or indirectly, has a living relationship. Thus, what is said in the Bible is expressed in categories
pertaining to material things (*das Dingliche*) or what is
available (*das Vorhandene*), whereas what is intended is to
say something about human existence. What is said in the
Bible has therefore to be interpreted in existentialistic terms in
order to make room for the existential decision of faith.[14]
What cannot be interpreted in an existentialistic manner falls
away—it is simply the mode of expression of the essential
datum, which means that it has nothing to do with faith.

What is quite clear, however, is that the presupposition underlying Bultmann's distinction between what is said and what is intended is a dilemma, a choice between "objectivity" and "existentiality," in which objectivity is understood in the Cartesian, neo-Kantian sense as that which the human mind has laid hold of and taken into its possession, something that is at man's disposal, like material *things*. In legitimate reaction to this, a purely existential interpretation of the Bible is in fact the only way out of the dilemma. It could nonetheless have been learned from Heidegger, the philosopher behind the whole of modern theology (and thus comparable to Aristotle, the philosopher who, via Arabic philosophy, was behind the whole of the "new theology" of the Middle Ages) that the presupposed dilemma is false and that there is a wonder, the event of Being, by which not only everything is what it is and is given to us, but also by which man exists in the mode of thinking and understanding.

The thesis that there is no separate theological hermeneutics, that "the interpretation of the biblical texts is subject to conditions of understanding which are no different from those of all other literature"[15] is characteristic of Bultmann's hermeneutics. The existentialistic interpretation of man's being provided Bultman not only with the "correct conceptual framework"[16] for his interpretation of history, of the New Testament and of dogmatic and theological statements, but also with the correct concepts for preaching. If, then, hermeneutics in theology are merely a question of science,[17] it is therefore relevant to ask for the "correct philosophy." [18] Bultmann found this philosophy in (the younger) Heidegger, at least in the sense that he found the *existentialia* of man's being in (the younger) Heidegger as formal structures of existence.[19] Certainly going contrary to (especially the later) Heidegger's intention—it is possible to criticize Bultmann's "existentialistic interpretation" in this connection already[20]—Bultmann concluded that the existentialistic interpretation (Heidegger's *Existenzial-interpretation*) of human existence as such belongs to the sphere of philosophy, whereas the authentically existential understanding (*das existenzielle Selbstverstandnis*), in the sense of personal choice and decision, belongs to the sphere of faith and preaching.[21] This latter existential decision of faith does not presuppose philosophical knowledge, whereas the former existentialistic interpretation is of decisive importance to our understanding of the Bible. The criterion for an authentic interpretation of the kerygma is therefore, in Bultmann's opinion, to be found in man himself, in his present understanding of himself as preunderstanding.[22] In other words, the hermeneutical principle is not contained in faith, but in human preunderstanding which, however, submits itself to the correction of the word of God. The Christian revelation therefore only discloses the "that" (*das Daß*) of previously given human contents—it says that, out of many existential possibilities, this and no other has been and is announced to us in Christ. Revelation is "address" (*Anrede*) and, in the believer, pure "event" (*Ereignis*). As a consequence of this view, several people have already maintained that a separate theological faculty is an absurdity and that theology should be a branch of the faculty of "philosophy and literature," because, in its interpretation of faith, theology recognizes no other scientific law than that of the exegesis and the interpretation of texts in general (applied in this case to the Bible, confessional texts and so on).

New scientific studies, such as those by H.-G. Gadamer, P. Ricoeur and the school of H. Diem—in addition to Diem himself,[23] especially Lothar Steiger[24]—have, in my opinion sufficiently demonstrated that theology has in fact no language of its own. According to these scholars, it speaks the same language as every man in the world and, for this reason, its rules are also those of universally human intelligibility. There is consequently no separate "theological" hermeneutics—hermeneutics is "neutral" with regard to faith in man's scientific understanding of Scripture, because the presupposition of this understanding is our question about ourselves. These recent studies have also shown, on the other hand, that this question discloses itself as God's question to us and that, on the basis of its own object, theology has a distinctive and irreducible relationship to this universal intelligibility. Theology is therefore not a particular case within one general "species," nor is it an isolated and as it were miraculous case without any relationship to universally human intelligibility. To express this in a different way, theology speaks a universally intelligible language—its principles are the universal hermeneutical principles of all human understanding—but theology does not deduce its intelligibility from these universal principles.

It is here that the "hermeneutical differentiation of theology" is situated, and it is precisely this which raises the question about the conditions which make *theological* understanding possible. The theological use of hermeneutics implies a *dogmatic* problem—dogmatic theology, faith, does not come exclusively within the sphere of *general* hermeneutics. Hermeneutics and dogmatics are not identical, yet they are inseparably linked. Without faith, there is no understanding of faith, but without understanding there is also no faith. P. Ricoeur in particular has shown, in a clear analysis, that "truth" is not obtainable separately, but is always in correlation to the adopted pattern of reading or the scientific model.[25] That is why there are as many different levels of objectivity and of truth as there are scientific models of reading—the concept of truth is multi-dimensional. If the theological pattern of reading is *reduced* to an "existentialistic interpretation," as found, in Bultmann's opinion, in Heidegger's "existentialistic analysis of being," which was completely "formalized" by Bultmann to neutral existentialistic basic categories that are open on all sides, there is a risk that the pattern of reading of our understanding of faith will be restricted. Bultmann avoids this danger because, as the believing Christian that he is and wishes to be, he is *inconsistent* in his own program of interpretation. Hence his Christian faith preserves him from some of the consequences at least of his own theology.

The Problem for the Catholic Faith

The Catholic theologian is also aware of the hermeneutical problem presented by the Bible, magisterial pronouncements and the tradition of faith, although he is probably conscious of the opposite question as of even greater urgency—the hermeneutical problem as a *dogmatic* matter. In the Catholic practice of the "development of dogma," a mass of hermeneutical material has been collected experientially, but Catholic theologians have practically never brought this hermeneutical material that is actually present in their own Church to light or attempted to thematize its content. Part of the reason for this has been a rather careless interpretation of one of the canons of the Council of Trent which was believed to have laid down the following hermeneutical principles for Catholics: "Ecclesia, cuius est iudicare de vero sensu et *interpretatione* Scripturarum sanctarum" ("It is the Church's prerogative to judge the true sense and *interpretation* of the Sacred

Scriptures").[26] Actually, this statement does not in any sense
imply that the Church's apostolic office is the *hermeneutical*
principle. What it does say is that this office is the judge of our
hermeneia or interpretation of faith and the Bible. The relationship between the "calling to mind" of the Holy Spirit,
who guides the Church in her unanimous confession of faith,
and the faith of the whole community of the Church together
with the magisterial pronouncements of the apostolic office
(which functions in the community as a *diākonia* and is, at
the same time, the judging, authentic exponent of the whole
faith of the Church) is undoubtedly a datum which the Catholic must take into account in his hermeneutics as a *dogmatic*
problem.

It would, however, be naive to assume that this solves the
hermeneutical question: it does no more than simply raise
the question. This is, of course, generally applicable—the author of a historical text may be completely trustworthy and
we may have absolute confidence in him, but precisely *what*
he is saying to us needs to be understood interpretatively. A
text is a document, the real meaning of which can only be
understood beyond its literal meaning because it tells us about
something, a "matter," which we too are trying to understand
and about which we ask questions in the light of our present-
day experience. This applies equally to conciliar texts and
other magisterial statements, even though a believer has complete confidence in these declarations. The magisterial statement may in certain cases (according to the subtle distinc-
tions of the First Vatican Council) even be infallible, but the
important point is to know precisely what (maybe in an infallible way) is said to me in that statement. *What* precisely
is expressed and to what can we and may we bind ourselves

in obedience to faith? The fact is that whole volumes of commentary have to be written in order to establish what the Council of Trent, for example, meant; a whole series of articles to enable us to know precisely in what respect the Church's apostolic office binds believers to the word of God. The interpreter is, after all, in history himself. Our patterns of reading are different now and our questions are different from those answered by the Fourth Lateran Council, for example, when it spoke of angels and devils or by the Council of Trent when it spoke of original sin and the Eucharist. And the answer to the questions asked in the thirteenth or the sixteenth century—in other words, the literal repetition even of unambiguously dogmatic definitions, such as those of Trent —is not an answer to our contemporary problems in which we are trying to come to an understanding of faith. Without the *Tridentine* answer to *my questions now,* I shall not understand what Trent means and my obedience in faith will fail to be authentic, so that a short-circuit will inevitably occur. Anyone who maintains—as some do—that Trent, because it is formulating a *dogma,* is, in what it explicitly says (*das Gesagte*), *a priori* an answer to my present-day questions is radically misconceiving the historicity of man's existence, of human questioning and of all human understanding. Authentic orthodoxy is seldom to be found in those who simply repeat literally what has already been said, with Denzinger in their hands as material to prove their point. Fortunately, however, their Christian faith transcends the inauthenticity of such thematic orthodoxy. A modern theologian, on the other hand, may feel *secure* as a believer and yet *hesitant* as a theologian —in this, he is respecting the mystery. One is sometimes bound to wonder whether the certainty of some theologians does not conceal a hesitant *faith.*

SOME HERMENEUTICAL PRINCIPLES

Today the question is being asked on all sides: Where are we free and where are we bound? Or can our freedom partly reach back to the past and can it even take hold of the past and thus, reinterpreting it, understand it? Is our being bound given precisely *in* this freedom?

The hermeneutical problem—since time immemorial, the problem of bridging the gap between the text and the reader —has come to a head in our own times. Indeed, the identity of faith, the problem of the relationship between Scripture and present-day preaching by the Church, is at stake. Can we and may we simply go on repeating word-for-word the "old" material, the Bible and the traditional statements, including those of the official *magisterium* of the Church in the present and the past, under the penalty of being unfaithful to the message if we do otherwise? Or is not just such a literal repetition itself unfaithful—is *development* in dogma, an interpretative contemporary translation of the "old" material of the faith, not essentially the fidelity that follows from man's historicity? If it is, how can this be done without being false to the gospel and to the Church which lives from the gospel? What, then, are the hermeneutical principles for this interpretative translation, this reinterpretation?

I cannot, within the limits of this chapter, deal with the many aspects of the modern problem of hermeneutics. While preparing a wider study of the subject, I will, however, touch upon one—in my view, fundamental—aspect of the problem, that of the historical dimension of our existence as believers, the very root of hermeneutics. Within the hermeneutics of history, I will further concentrate on only one aspect, that of the hermeneutical significance of the *distance in time* in what we may call *"historical* interhuman encounter" (in contrast to a *direct* encounter in dialogue with a fellow human-being, but within what is essentially the same noetic pattern of "interhuman" encounter)—in fact, then, our encounter with the human witness to faith that we find in Scripture, in the whole of tradition, in conciliar texts and so on. What, then, is the hermeneutical significance of this distance in time for our understanding of what is expressed in those texts as a call to us as well, people living in the twentieth century? It will become clear why living orthodoxy can be attained only *within* a reinterpretative present-day understanding of faith which is faithful to the biblical interpretation of faith. We can, after all, never dispense with interpretation of a previously given (and originally, a biblical) interpretation, which becomes authentically understood precisely in the reinterpretation. In this examination of the problem, I will consider three aspects of the "hermeneutics of history."

The Past in the Light of the Present

The specific objectivity that is peculiar to the interpretation of history is partly determined by the distance in time between the past and the present.[27] This distance, after all, is not a void, but an event that is also our past—the distance is filled by the continuity of tradition. The present, from which we question the past (for example, the Bible or the declarations of the Council of Trent), has partly been formed by the past that lies between the Bible or the Council of Trent and the present. From this present, the interpretation of history gives a name and a meaning to the past that it is seeking to understand, a name which it could not have had when it was itself the present. The classical example is well-known—a period which could not have been called the "Middle Ages" when it was the living present is now (provisionally) called this by us on the basis of the distance in time which separates us from it. This name has its basis in that period itself, and yet this period has only been called the "Middle Ages" since our re-interpretation in the light of our present. The *same* thing is seen *differently*. The past when it was present (for example, the time of the Council of Trent) itself had then a past (the memory—the being in a tradition—of the people of that time) and a future (the future of that time, formed by expectations, perspectives of things to come, anxieties, ignorance and so on). But from *our* present, with our *much longer* past since Trent and the past which was present at that time, together with our recent past and our own future, all this stands in a different light—what was the future of *that* past is already partly past for us. We can now therefore appraise the *distinctive* meaning of *that* (Tridentine) past and show it in a different light.

This involves a serious tension. Anyone wishing to understand a Tridentine canon or a New Testament text, for example, has to transfer himself into the past—in his inquiry he must take as his central point of reference people who are different from his contemporaries and strange to him, and a past period. This should not be understood in the romantic sense of a Schleiermacher, for example, as though we could enter intimately into the spiritual lives of the Tridentine fathers or of Paul and thus "reconstruct" the past—that past is a fact and it is unrepeatable and cannot be reconstructed. It means rather that the modern reader should transfer *himself,* together with all his present-day belongings, and make the perspective within which the earlier writer formed his view his own. The reader or interpreter never simply reads the literal text, but always interprets, even if he is only reading a banal little novel. In so doing, however, he has to allow the objective integrity of what the earlier writer said to prevail, to be open and obedient to the authority of the text. This applies both to the interpretation of profane literature, such as the writings of Plato or Aristotle, and to the interpretation of the Bible. The meaning of the text is normative in every understanding of a text. But the interpreter's submission to the text is bound to take place within the context of assumptions and ideas formed by the present in which he lives, that present which has itself been formed by a much larger past than the past of the Tridentine or the biblical text. He cannot put this reality—the filled distance in time—"in brackets." But this is unnecessary, and it is not even permissible since it would make an authentic understanding of the text, in its dimension of reaching towards the future, impossible. Without the voice of the present it is impossible to understand the past in its own distinctive—and hence different—quality.

I am not so much asserting here that a preunderstanding is necessary *because* this preunderstanding is necessary to all understanding. What I do maintain is that a preunderstanding (which is *in fact* always involved) that is the product of conscious reflection is indispensable to any understanding that is to be scientifically justified. Thus, for example, the special characteristics of seventeenth-century French spirituality are difficult to understand apart from the future development of the situation which became reality in the eighteenth century. It is only the French Enlightenment, as a reaction, which enables us to see clearly the distinctive quality of the seventeenth century in France. The distance in time, which was often characterized in the past as an obstacle to objective interpretation of texts and of history that had to be overcome, is now

seen rather as the ontological condition that makes this interpretation possible. Critics such as P. Ricoeur, R. Aron, H.
Marrou and H. G. Gadamer are all in agreement with this
and M. Heidegger has revealed the ontological pre-structures
of this historical insight.

It is precisely this distance in time, the filled "interim" between, for example, the Council of Trent and our own period,
which evokes the hermeneutical problem. Ultimately, it *is* the
hermeneutical problem. How can a being, personally involved
in history, understand history in a *historical* manner? Ricoeur
has formulated the problem more clearly than anyone else:
How can human life, expressing itself, objectivize itself (for
example, in a text) and, consequently, how does human life,
objectivizing itself in this way, call meanings into being which
can later be taken up again and understood by another historical being in a different historical situation?[28] Hermeneutics points to what enables us to listen to the meaning of
the message which comes to us from the utterances of men
in the past.[29] As we have already seen, the distance in time
is not something that has to be spanned, but a positive condition that makes it possible for us to understand the past
precisely as the past. That is why, on generally hermeneutical
grounds, scripture (which, as a text, also has a future-dimension of its own) cannot be understood if the tradition of faith
which has grown out of it is neglected. Biblicism is condemned
in advance by the very historicity of our existence and our understanding. Historical objectivity is the truth of the past *in the
light of the present* and not a reconstruction of the past in its
unrepeatable factuality. Simply to repeat the earlier formulae
of faith word-for-word is to misconceive the historicity of our
existence as men and is therefore a grave danger to genuinely
biblical orthodoxy. No one can dissociate himself from the

spirit of the age in which he is living and from the living questions which arise from it. It is from his own period that a man questions the past. Hence every age rewrites history and sees the *same* past quite *differently,* and it is possible for the reader of history to savor the distinctive quality not only of the period being studied and interpreted but of the period in which the history is being written. The historicist or positivist, in whose view the texts should be allowed to speak for themselves—"objectively"—without any modern presuppositions, without being placed in the light of the present, sees a failure of objectivity in all this. To a utopian positivism of that kind Gadamer (and Marrou as well) has rightly objected, saying that if this is a shortcoming, we are still bound to reflect on this inevitable fact, since it could well point to a structural principle.[30]

It is, after all, impossible to take an abstract ideal of truth as one's point of departure. As we have already seen, the concepts of objectivity and truth cannot be taken separately but must always be seen in correlation with the scientific model concerned, or the pattern of reading that one has decided for oneself. That is why it is necessary to discover the transcendental condition that makes history possible from the *quaestio facti* (the subjectivity in the interpretation of history which is a matter of fact)—in other words, to find out, "in fundamental generality," [31] *what* is implied by the fact that the contemporary point of view of the reader and his situation in life are always, inevitably echoed in every textual interpretation. In this way, one avoids forming an ideal of scientifically justified interpretation of the past in the abstract and *a priori,* but makes an attempt to find out how it is *de facto* possible to understand the past.

Everyone agrees that anyone who wants to understand a

text must be ready to submit to the authority of that text and should not impose his own meaning on it. Textual interpretation should never become inegesis. The text itself is binding and acts as a norm to understanding. This is based on general hermeneutical principles (and not on, for example, biblical "inspiration") and applies to every text—whether scriptural, conciliar or a passage from profane literature. A hermeneutically trained thinker must *a priori* be open to the deviation of the text from his own views, demands and expectations. What is thematically new in modern hermeneutics is our having come to realize that this openness is made possible not by our adopting a neutral attitude and putting our own background in brackets in an effort to exclude it, but only by our doing the direct opposite—quite consciously admitting the light that we can throw on the text in question from our own contemporary situation. The exclusion of the presuppositions and prejudgments (that is, prior judgments) which we all have because we are situated in history and live from the past in the present towards a future does not involve the elimination of these presuppositions altogether; on the contrary, we should remain *conscious* of the fact that we approach the text from a preunderstanding and that we must, in so doing, *confront* that text with our own preunderstanding. The process of understanding is accomplished precisely in the possible *correction* of our preunderstanding. In the understanding of faith, which is subject to God's speaking to us, this correction of our preunderstanding is of a very special nature, but in its formal structures it follows the general hermeneutical pattern. It is precisely those presuppositions which we have not made conscious (but which are nonetheless always present) which make us blind to, or screen us from, a right understanding of, say, the texts of the Council of Trent. Prejudgment does not in itself have an unfavorable meaning. Its positive content reveals it as a necessary structural aspect of all understanding.[32]

The insight that man is, because of his historicity, *in a tradition* and that his freedom is limited, among other things, by the factuality of this past is therefore fundamental to hermeneutics. He does, however, understand the past creatively in the light of the present. It belongs to man's very being to be within a tradition while re-activating it,[33] and there is a living tradition only if, in the light of the present that is orientated towards the future, what has already found expression is reinterpreted towards the future. But the question is, which presuppositions are legitimate and which are illegitimate in this light of the present? This is something that the interpreter cannot determine for himself. It is a question that can be answered only in the understanding itself, in the dialogue with the other—in this case, with the text. Thanks to the distance in time between, for example, the Council of Trent and our present, we can understand the Council of Trent in the light of this present. Thanks too to this distance, which is filled by the continuity of tradition, we can make a distinction in our understanding between legitimate and illegitimate prejudgments. It is precisely in selecting legitimate from among illegitimate presuppositions that our understanding of the Council of Trent takes place and that we are obedient, in the light of the present, to the authority of the Tridentine text. Understanding outside a tradition is humanly inconceivable, since such an understanding involves a fundamental misconception of the ontological prestructure and of the condition that makes all human understanding possible. On the basis of our essential being as men, understanding is a *reinterpretative understanding of tradition*—an understanding of tradition in the manner of reinterpretation.

Submitting to the Tridentine text means, therefore, that a *question* is addressed to the text itself and that an answer is expected to this question from the text. Our continued openness to new possibilities is expressed in this question. It does not in any sense mean that we obliterate our whole preunderstanding and allow the other (that is, the text) to pre-empt our consciousness. It means that we, in the awareness of our own historicity, consciously approach the traditional text and thus, at the same time taking account of our own historicity, read the text.

The important conclusion to be drawn from this is that all understanding has the present existential experience as its hermeneutical situation. The interpreter is involved in this situation, is so much a part of it that he can never fully think it out or come to a clear understanding of it in his own mind. We must therefore first of all bring this hermeneutical situation into consciousness if we are to understand any traditional text. In so doing, we produce the frame of reference in which questions can be asked and an answer expected from tradition. The author of the traditional text had, of course, his own frame of reference in which he asked questions, but this does not mean that to reach historical understanding we have to transfer ourselves from our own sphere to that of the author, as historicism claims to be able to do. There are not two closed spheres, the author's and our own. From our own sphere, we understand *ourselves,* together with others in the present or from the past. Truth is brought to light only within human intersubjectivity. Language is therefore always essential if reality is to be reflected in truth. Assent to truth is accomplished in dialogue with people both of the present and from the past. The tension of the initial distance between the present and the past should not, therefore, be bridged. Hermeneutics requires us to design a *historical* frame of reference which is distinct from our *present* frame of reference and thus to become conscious of the other as different within the fusion of the two spheres (since historicity is one great evolving process)—that is understanding the past.[34] Our designing of a historical frame of reference is therefore only a phase in the accomplishment of understanding, a phase that is over as soon as we reach the sphere of understanding of the present. It is only in this way that the whole interpretation of Scripture in the line of the history of the transmission of traditions is explicable—new levels of tradition have been deposited on earlier levels, reinterpreting the earlier levels of tradition in the light of their own present. All that we have is this final editing.

The importance of the present as the hermeneutical situation is clear, for example, in the difference between the Old Testament interpretation and the Christian interpretation of the same Old Testament texts. In both cases, the Old Testament remained unchanged and valid as a sacred book, but the Christians reread and reinterpreted the Old Testament in the light of the new hermeneutical situation (the eschatological kerygma of Christianity). The New Testament thus found itself in a different frame of reference from the one which the Jews, or an Old Testament scholar, would take as their basis. In this way, a distinction between the Old Testament and the New Testament understanding of the same Old Testament books came into being. The New Testament texts were, after all, to a great extent only the literary expression of a Christian rereading of the Old Testament in the light of the new hermeneutical situation—the encounter with Jesus, the Lord. Even within the New Testament itself, a theological process of reinterpretative understanding of initial Christian interpretations took place on the basis of the gradually chang-

ing social context of the earliest Church. The difference that
is apparent between the translation of the Septuagint and the
earlier Hebrew texts is equally indicative of the importance
of the socio-cultural context as a hermeneutical situation. We
have here in two distinct texts what can be separated in the
synoptic "history of traditions" only by comparison and
analysis of the three synoptic gospels—earlier, normative *logia,*
dialogues and texts are reinterpreted in, and in the light of,
a new context in life. This is an ordinary human hermeneutical
process *within* the life of the Church. For a Christian, however, the eschatological kerygma of Christ is a situation that
is constant and cannot be superseded. That is why it acts as a
constant norm to every age's understanding of biblical faith—
the identity in faith must therefore be preserved *within* the
Christian reinterpretation itself.

The result of this analysis is extremely important. It is that
understanding of a traditional text takes place only in its
application to the present, and not in a kind of interpretation
"in itself," in a historical reconstruction or in a return to the
original period. Christian understanding of the Bible is therefore different from what is known simply as exegesis. If an
earlier truth is to be preserved in accordance with its original
intention, it must be reformulated in the light of the present
and interpreted differently. With reference to Jesus' logion
that what God has joined together, no man must put asunder,
for example, the text of Matthew 19.1–9 said that a man may
not divorce his wife. In Oriental and Jewish society a wife was
never allowed to take the initiative and divorce her husband.
In Greco-Roman society, on the other hand, the situation was
different—according to hellenistic custom women as well as
men were able to take the initiative. The formulation of this
truth was consequently revised, brought up to date and trans-

lated into contemporary terms, so as to preserve the intention of the logion in its pure form in the new social environment. Therefore, according to Mark 10.10-12 Jesus said that neither the husband *nor the wife* may divorce. A literal repetition of the earlier formulation of the truth would have been most ambiguous in the new situation, since an initiative taken by the wife to divorce her husband would have been regarded as legitimate, and this would have been flagrantly contrary to the deepest intention of the original statement. It was only in this contemporary application—in the reinterpretation, in other words—that it was clear that Christians had genuinely understood the "earlier" truth. Similarly, our understanding of the Tridentine dogma of transubstantiation comes about, not in a literal repetition of the dogma, but in a contemporary interpretation and a new formulation. On the basis of the filled distance in time, a text is understood only if it is understood in a *different* way—which does not mean a better or a worse way—from the way in which it was understood in its past social and cultural context. Understanding must change in changing situations, otherwise the same thing cannot continue to be understood.

Understanding is therefore intimately bound to the text which has to be understood. The text has a normative value, but we can understand it only in its application to the present. Exposition of the text may never replace the text itself, but the historical survival of the tradition (the text) consists in a new appropriation which of necessity takes place again and again. The past will remain unintelligible to us if we do not incorporate its meaning into our contemporary existential experience. If we do not do this, we shall not understand what the past really has to say to us. But the fact that our present frame of reference inevitably plays a part in our interpretation of an earlier text does not mean that we can first enter completely into the life of the past, so as to understand it, and only then, as it were in the second place, translate the result into terms of our present frame of reference. The two phases run parallel to each other, and our understanding is a product of their interaction. The task of interpretation therefore involves finding the right phraseology to convey the real, essential meaning of the text, as there is no interpretation which "in itself"—that is, independent of human concepts— holds good for all historical periods. It is within the context of the present, with its particular insights, that the traditional text finds its own inner fulfillment. Our productive creativity and our bond with tradition therefore interact in forming our understanding of the text, since in bringing his present understanding to bear on a traditional text the interpreter is not free with respect to the distinctive meaning of the text but is bound to it. We can say that by definition tradition receives from the interpreter of another age a different reading from the one called for by the texts in themselves. Bultmann's distinction between "what is said" and "what is intended" is simply insufficient to explain what occurs here, since the divine truth which the author of the traditional text intended to express must somehow (however inadequately) be expressed in the text. But this "intended meaning" is included in a meaning which has not yet been consciously perceived by the author himself and has still to be unveiled—a meaning, that is, which is implicit in everything that is expressed in this "saying and intending" and which discloses itself without having been thematically intended.

I am thinking here, for example, of the book in which J. B. Metz[35] analyzed the basic form of Thomas's philosophical and theological thought—a datum which was really present

in Thomas's texts, but of which he himself was not thematically conscious, can only in the light of the present be set
free and given the meaning which was objectively present
but which was not explicitly recognized for centuries. Aside
from these partly implied aspects, there is always fundamentally that which is "not thought of," which *gives us to
think,* but is itself never thought: "What is not thought is the
supreme gift that any thinking has to give."[36]

Taking the texts themselves as his point of departure, the interpreter therefore goes beyond the texts and their meaning and en-
quires about the *reality* to which the texts intentionally or unin-
tentially bear witness.[37] What do the texts say and to what reality
do they testify? These two questions are not entirely separate,
nor are they completely identical. What is said is already an
interpretation of the reality. Reinterpretation would therefore
seem to be necessary wherever unrest and doubt is occasioned
by what is "directly said" or a feeling of strangeness is caused
by the "distance in time" which separates us from these texts
—although this does not mean that our living relationship
with the reality that is expressed in the texts is thereby broken.
What is "unintelligible" in the text calls for reinterpretative
understanding. *Hermeneia* is, after all, literally an "interpretation" of something that comes to us in a "foreign language." We aim to appropriate its meaning, make it our own,
through the interpretation. The hermeneutical basis for this
is the living relationship which we ourselves have with the
same matter or reality that is discussed in the text. The preunderstanding from which we approach the text, therefore, is
already implied in this living relationship. This applies in all
cases—to the understanding of the Bible or of any conciliar
text. Bultmann rightly recognized this. Catholic theology
regards it as an essential structural element of the development

of dogma. It is, after all, not in the first place a doctrine about the Eucharist that is handed down to us, but the eucharistic reality itself—we celebrate the Eucharist in our contemporary Christian experience. Existentially involved in this celebration of the Eucharist, and thus in the light of the celebration and the preunderstanding that is given in it, we enquire into the earlier texts of the Bible, the Council of Trent and so on, which bear witness to the same reality. In this context, it should not be forgotten that such a preunderstanding is already inwardly *Christian,* that it is already within the sphere of faith. Understanding the Bible and understanding Trent is therefore always a *suntheologein,* allowing the reality of salvation to speak in discourse with the other (who is present either in person or in a text). The truth comes to light only in intersubjectivity, and whether this takes place in a dialogue with a living person or with a text belonging to a period long past seems to me to make no essential difference. For purely hermeneutical reasons, therefore, my present-day understanding in faith cannot take place outside this dialogue with Scripture and the whole tradition of faith.

Anyone who tries to think as a solipsist, purely in the light of his own present existential experience, is fundamentally misjudging the "human predicament," in his being as a believer as well—he is closing the doors which lead to the kingdom of truth. Human freedom is not suspended in a vacuum—it is both in a tradition and situated in contemporary experience. As Bultmann, echoing Heidegger, rightly said, freedom is exercised in the present with a look towards the future. But the past, although it is unrepeatable in its factuality, also contains an element which transcends factuality. We stand in a present which is the future, realizing itself now, of what was once, in time gone by, the present, but is now the past. The past itself has its own future-dimension. The old controversy about the *sensus litteralis* and the *sensus plenior* of Scripture and the ecumenical problem of the relationship between dogma (in the Catholic sense) and Scripture are given unexpected perspectives in the light of Heidegger's "hermeneutics of factuality." What is at stake is the future of Scripture itself. The meaning of the past is fulfilled in the present and the future by our freedom. The past will always display itself again and again in the light of the present and, what is more, it will display itself again and again differently. And, in this, the present is not only the future-dimension of the past, but also, like every human period, a moment of God's grace.

Both the Present and the Past within the Sphere of the Promise

When we have said this, it does not mean that we are finished with the hermeneutics of history, as the exponents of the so-called "new hermeneutics," whose inspiration is exclusively confined to the *hermeneia* of the humanities, one-sidedly believe, thus distorting hermeneutics precisely in what it positively affirms.

The new hermeneutics (especially that of Bultmann, the post-Bultmannians and Gadamer) are one-sided because they question only those human existential possibilities *that have already been brought to expression*. They do not question what is, from the biblical point of view, of primary importance —the future possibilities, what is new and completely *unprecedented*. The biblical primacy of the future over the present and the past is passed over in silence. Pannenberg[38] and Moltmann[39] have rightly protested against this. Every interpretation of the past in the light of the present is, after all, open to the future and orientated towards it. The future is not, of course, to be interpreted, but it certainly has to be realized and, what is more, it should bring something new into being. Every dogma must have an orientation towards the future and be open to the sphere of the future. This has consequences for our conception of dogma itself, since truth then becomes, for us now, something whose fullness belongs to the future; to the extent that its content is already realized, it discloses itself as essentially a *promise*. The present, itself a sphere of interpretation of the past, must be caught up in a sphere of promise, or the past will not be seen clearly for what it is. What is ultimately and primarily in question here is conceiving both the present and the past as open-ended, orientated towards a new reality—what is still to come. Dogma thus becomes the proclamation of the historical realization of God's promise, which of its very nature implies an openness to the future and to new historical realizations.[40]

Everything to which the Bible bears witness is directed towards the fulfillment in the future of God's promise, the history of which has been narrated in faith in the Bible. It is possible to express our understanding of the Bible in this way—we should not look back at the Bible, but rather look forward, with the Bible, to a future which is given to us to be achieved—to be achieved, but also *given us* to be achieved. What Bultmann has called the "Woraufhin," what biblical interpretation "points to," cannot, in the last resort, therefore be what Bultmann meant it to be; it must be orthodoxy (the correct interpretation of the promise insofar as it has already been realized in the past) as the basis of the orthopraxis whereby the promise realizes a new future in us. It is only in the sphere of action—of doing in the faith—that orthodox interpretation can be inwardly fulfilled. The new hermeneutics has lost sight of the fact that the *traditum* is not simply a text, or existential possibilities that are simply expressed within it. It is more than a closed *depositum* on which we draw again and again in the light of the present. There certainly is a "deposit of faith," but its content still remains, on the basis of the promise already realized in Christ (realized in fact, but nonetheless still really a *promise*), a promise-for-us, with the result that interpretation becomes "hermeneutics of praxis."[41] The Bible reminds us of God's faithfulness in the past, precisely in order to arouse our confidence in God's faithfulness in the future. What occurred in the past has canonical value for the community of believers who are orientated towards the future. God will be in the future as he was in the past and is now, always unexpectedly new.

Since Bultmann, however, primacy has been accorded in the "new hermeneutics" not to the future, but to the narrow point of the present. History and interpretation would therefore seem to reach their final end in our present, which is then regarded as the *eschaton* of all *meaning* and the real, determining hermeneutical principle. Such hermeneutics de-eschatologizes history by raising the present itself to the level of *eschaton*. All tension towards a future in which real salvation-history is still possible and the promise is still being realized is thus annihilated, or else history is made the paradoxical counterpart of Christian life—Christian existence is then the "end of human history," an eschatological mode of existence *in* human history, which continues, but is not redeemed *as* history. Authentic existence is thus dissociated both from nature and from history. This seems to me to be one of the fundamental errors of the "existentialistic interpretation" of the Bible—it has tried, too one-sidedly, to associate itself with the hermenutics of the humanities. This is also Gadamer's basic failing. But it is not interpretation which has the last word, but orthopraxis, making everything new by virtue of God's promise. It is a question of being orientated towards the grace of the future, remembering God's promise and being active in faith and, in so doing, *making* dogma true. The profession of faith and dogma, after all, proclaim a future which must be realized in hope and is therefore not exclusively the object of contemplation but a task to be accomplished. Ultimately it is only in and through this historical realization that dogma is interpreted authentically and that the identity of the faith is, thanks to God's promise, guaranteed in continuing history. The object of faith is God, who in Christ is man's future.

Permanence in the Present, Past and Future

Finally, there is also a third aspect of the hermeneutics of history. The "new hermeneutics," not only that of the post-Bultmannians and of the philosopher Gadamer but also that of Pannenberg and Moltmann, suffers from still another fundamental shortcoming. In my opinion, this is because these thinkers have lost sight of another decisive aspect of man's temporality—that is, of the fact that our historicity involves not only lived temporality but also consciousness of time. This consciousness of time, which can also, of its nature, be conceptualized, implies a certain transcendence of temporality— at least lived temporality. This does not mean that we are in some way able to escape from time, capable of taking a kind of bird's eye view of truth or of receiving it into a consciousness (however restricted) wholly detached from history, and to preserve the identity of the faith in this way. Even that is not granted to historical man on earth. But it does imply a real *openness* in our temporality, something which could almost be called (if the phrase were not too strong) a "trans-historical" element, although this cannot be positively defined or isolated for consideration. The past is within the present on the way towards the future, which then, in its turn, via the present, fades into the past—a course which leads from interpretation to doing and then reinterpretation. In this fluidity in the development of tradition there is, in other words, an aspect of permanence, a dynamic self-identity which cannot in itself be expressed. The objective *perspective* of faith, which is not in itself thematic and cannot be conceptualized, is thus to some extent brought to light and expressed *in* reinterpretation as it were by a circuitous route (via the interpretative aspect of the act of faith), with the consequence that it becomes a power for action which is directed towards the future. Extending Heidegger's idea to the sphere of theology, it is possible to say that an intellectual grasp of faith is possible if we are "obedient to the mute voice of being,"[42] since revelation is in the first place a living reality which approaches us, and the understanding we reach in faith is not purely a description of existence or a human project for the future: it is a response to an appeal which is objective, or real.

Is our faith, then, so far as its content is concerned, always provisional, conditional—a hypothesis? Such an attitude would be human, but it would fail to take the "human predicament" really into account. One would not want to live in the present, simply because one was aware of a future which would be different. I would like to set against this erroneous concept of human temporality the idea that there are no formulae of faith which are, as formulae, enduringly valid, capable of transmitting the living faith to men of all ages. Is this relativism? Not at all. It is what is meant by the identity of the faith with itself *in history*. For we do not possess the absolute which acts as an inner norm to our faith in an absolute way; we possess it only within our historical situation.

As pilgrims on the way, we live historically in the absolute, orientated towards the absolute, because this absolute embraces us in grace, without our being able to embrace it. Is there, then, no precise content of faith? Of course there is. But there is no explicitly fixed *representation* of truth—which is not the same thing. Faith becomes meaningless without content, and it would become meaningless too if this content of faith were susceptible of constant change. But the inviolable aspect of the content of faith is situated in an inexpressible *objective perspective* which is again and again meaningfully suggested from and in a changing historical outline and which makes itself felt *in* every historical outline—the mystery is always giving us to *think*. In their explicitly conceptual content, the dynamics of our understanding of faith are therefore essentially active both in a demythologizing and in a "mythologizing" way, on the one hand demolishing earlier representations of the truths of faith and on the other constructing new concepts. The vital core of our knowledge in faith is never what is capable of being *fixed* conceptually, but our concepts are assuredly subject to its normative influence. The conceptuality which belongs to our thinking, and hence to our understanding of the faith, is subject to our situation in history. The real content of human knowing and believing is the ever present *mystery* of promise —the mystery which is not uttered, which is everywhere reaching towards expression but in itself is never thought. It is this which makes our understanding in faith, which is realized only through a conceptual (or even poetical) interpretation, a ceaseless and fascinating adventure—an experience like that of the believer in the Bible who touched the hem of Jesus' garment.

This view both accepts and at the same time limits pluralism in our expressions of faith. Pluralism in our interpretations of faith cannot, after all, be extended endlessly—at least, not in the sense that the mystery can be thought of as an *unknown* quantity, to be approached via infinitely divergent interpretations. This limitation of pluralism means of course that the truth of the mystery of faith must to some extent be present *in* the conceptualizations of faith, as an *aspect* of the total consciousness of faith, with the result that pluralism become an expression of unanimity on a deeper level and that a (collective) judgment about what does and what does not form part of orthodox faith really becomes possible, even though years or even centuries may pass (as the development of dogma clearly shows) before the Church is ready to make a decisive judgment in questions of faith.[43]

The thing which is of itself indefinable—the mystery of promise which gives itself in history—ensures the identity of the faith *in* the Church's successive interpretations of the faith. Nothing of this mystery is to be found in the new dogma of the anti-metaphysical trend, dominating all the significant theological thought today, which is premised on the narrow basis of the pure "event." It is absent, therefore, from the thinking of Bultmann and his school and even from that of Gadamer, whose thought is otherwise of such great subtlety; that he should arrive at "historical scepticism" as the only tenable position was a foregone conclusion—one which he in any case, as a Lutheran, regards as authentically Protestant.[44] If we attach to our concepts of the faith *only* the significance of historical expressions, we bid farewell to the *truth* which is always coming. In that event, "authenticity" ("it says something to me") is the final criterion which a man, even a believer, applies to his personal attitude—"authenticity" within a historical scepticism and within a religious formation themat-ically cut off from its source and its future. The inner conse-quence of this is ultimately a post-Christian, or atheistic, "Christianity" which is postulated with the same "dogmatic" certainty as characterized traditional theism in the past and which thinks of all "dissenters" as incorrigible "ecclesiastical conservatives"—the modern "anathema." But life, even Chris-tian life, is, thank God, always a greater force than theory. A theory may tempt us for a while, but at the same time it may act as a stimulus for us to reconsider what in the past seemed to be, from the Christian point of view, quite obvious.

Conclusion

I have tried to demonstrate in my analysis that we cannot, from where we stand, approach the traditional faith directly; we can do so only by passing, with an understanding illumined by faith, through the conceptual framework of "modernity." And in so doing, we *de facto* transcend this modernity—the hermeneutical situation of the present—interpreting and doing in faith, in an *act of surrender* in which our progress through time may really become a gradual realization of the *eschaton*. Shall we, then, always correctly interpret the mystery which embraces us, which is realizing itself and which compels us to express it interpretatively? As I have already said, the mystery which gives itself in history ensures the identity of the faith, but only on condition that we continue to listen faithfully and commit ourselves faithfully to the future. This continuity is not a destiny or a promise existing only in heaven. It is an event. Continuity is therefore not the result of a human plan, but it is nonetheless implicit in man's believing faithfulness.[45] The promise is actively present in *this*. Every personal reinter-

pretation and reformulation is not therefore in itself in accordance with the identity of the Christian faith, although a
false interpretation does not make someone who is in good
faith within the sphere of the Church "unchristian." There
are indeed false interpretations of the Christian faith. But my
only aim here has been to throw some light on the fact that we
should not be afraid of serious attempts to reinterpret the faith
and that the correctness of these interpretations cannot be
tested simply by setting earlier formulae of faith against them,
since these too always require interpretation and have still to
be *made* true. They themselves have once been an answer, and
have been understood as such, but an answer to a different
question.

It is precisely fidelity to the promise of the gospel, living in
the Church, that demands that we, twentieth-century men,
should reinterpret. This is, of course, a very hazardous undertaking. The New Testament authors themselves have already
set us an example in it, since what was their task in different
situations (and *certeris paribus*) is also our task now:—to
present the original Dialogue (a living prophecy!) again and
again, and above all to put it into action and to let it be heard
as the word of God in constantly changing situations in life. It
is only within the ecclesial sphere—resounding with the echo
of the promise—that Christian understanding is truly possible.
Hermeneutics and theology only perform a service in this—
they allow the unadulterated biblical message to be really
understandable in the present "hermeneutical situation." For
the Christian reality of faith is only brought to light and thus
brought to the *world* in dialogue with the Church—by the
Church as the *sacramentum mundi*. Theology is therefore an
ecclesial and apostolic undertaking within the Church in the
service of the world.

It is only in the unanimity of the whole community of the Church, guided and accompanied by the world episcopate in its unanimous interpretation of faith, together with the office of Peter as the keystone of the vault of the great *koinōnia* of the same faith, hope and love, that any new theological interpretation is authenticated as a contemporary understanding in faith by the hall-mark of the Holy Spirit, the living principle, always present here and now, of *anamnesis,* or calling to mind in faith and faithfulness to the gospel. This is also the point of departure for a new future, in confidence in the promise of God.

Notes

1. M. Heidegger, *Zur Seinsfrage,* Frankfurt a. M. (1956), p. 36.

2. By "existential" theology (with all its variations) I mean that theology, originally inspired by S. Kierkegaard and M. Heidegger, which takes human existence (however this is interpreted) as its point of departure and tries to understand it in terms of faith. Representative of this trend are, first, Bultmann, and after him especially H. Braun, E. Fuchs, G. Ebeling and H. Ott.

3. The "historical" theologians to whom I am referring here form the "Pannenberg" circle. Cf. *Theology as History* (New Frontiers in Theology, III), New York-Evanston-London (1967). History itself, in which no distinction can be made between profane history and the history of salvation, is the sphere of God's revelation. In contrast to existential theology, which is restricted to a pure theology of the "revelation of the word," historical theology concentrates on a theology of the history in which God's revelation of himself takes place in an indirect way. Dialogue between these two movements has scarcely commenced.

4. An analysis of the modern "loss of reality" has been provided by, among others, W. Weischedel, *Wirklichkeit und Wirklichkeiten,* Berlin (1960); especially Heidegger ("forgetfulness of being"), for example, *Die Technik und die Kehre,* Pfullingen (1962); cf. H. Freyer, *Theorie des gegenwärtigen Zeitalters,* Stuttgart (1955); P. Ricoeur, "Prévision économique et choix éthique," *Esprit* 34 (1966), pp. 178–93.

5. M. Heidegger, *Sein und Zeit,* Halle (1927, reprinted 1953), p. 32.

6. R. Bultmann, *Glauben und Verstehen* II, Tübingen (1952, ³1961), pp.

277 ff.; "Das Problem einer theologischen Exegese des Neuen Testaments," *Zwischen den Zeiten* 3 (1925), pp. 334–57; E. Fuchs, *Hermeneutik,* Bad Canstatt (³1963), pp. 118–26; G. Ebeling, especially "Die Anfänge von Luthers Hermeneutik," *Zeitschrift für Theologie und Kirche* 48 (1951), pp. 172–230.

7. P. Ricoeur, "Existence et herméneutique," *Interpretation der Welt* (Festschrift für R. Guardini), Würzburg (1965), pp. 32–51; "Hermeneutik der Symbole und philosophisches Denken," *Kerygma und Mythos* VI-1, Hamburg (1963), pp. 45–68, especially p. 54, where there is reference to the *Kreis der Hermeneutik* ("hermeneutical circle"): "One must understand in order to believe, but one must believe in order to understand." Cf. *id., De l'interprétation,* Paris (1966).

8. H.-G. Gadamer, *Wahrheit und Methode,* Tübingen (²1965), especially pp. 250 ff.

9. R. Tillich, *Systematische Theologie* I, Stuttgart (²1956), pp. 9 and 15 ff. among other places; K. Löwith, *Wissen, Glauben und Skepsis,* Göttingen (1956), pp. 18 ff.

10. R. Bultmann, *Kerygma und Mythos* II, Hamburg (1952), p. 191; see also II, p. 189.

11. See under "Dogma," *Theologisch Woordenboek,* Roermond (1952), pt. 1, col. 1079–80. The same distinction has also been made by Protestant theologians, especially since A. Harnack, *Lehrbuch der Dogmengeschichte,* pt. 1, Tübingen (⁴1909), p. 160. Elsewhere, in his *Grundriß der Dogmengeschichte,* Tübingen, (1898), p. 2, Harnack called the Catholic view of the development of dogma "the most impressive attempt to solve" this problem. Even the Church Fathers recognized the distinction between the "essence" and its "mode of expression"; see F. Overbeek, *Die Anfänge der patristischen Literatur* (²1954), p. 63.

12. E. Schillebeeckx, *Die eucharistische Gegenwart,* Dusseldorf (1967), pp. 15–18. English translation, *The Eucharist,* New York (Sheed and Ward), 1968.

13. R. Bultmann, among other places, "Das Problem einer theologischen Exegese des Neuen Testaments," *op. cit.* (footnote 2), p. 340; *Glauben und Verstehen,* Tübingen (1952, ³1961), pt. 2, pp. 211–35; pt. 3 (1960), pp. 142–50; see also E. Fuchs, *Zeitschrift für Theologie und Kirche* 58 (1961), p. 256.

14. R. Bultmann, among other places, *Glauben und Verstehen* III, pp. 107–21; *Jesus Christus und die Mythologie,* Hamburg (1964), pp. 50–68; "Zum Problem der Entmythologisierung," *Kerygma und Mythos* VI-1, Hamburg (1963), pp. 20–27.

15. R. Bultmann, _Glauben und Verstehen_ II, p. 231; I, p. 133. Bultmann formulated the fundamental principles of his hermeneutics ex professo in 1950; see "Das Problem der Hermeneutik," _Glauben und Verstehen_ II, pp. 211-35.

16. R. Bultmann in _Kerygma und Mythos_ II, Hamburg (1952), p. 189; briefly stated in _Jesus Christus und die Mythologie, op. cit.,_ pp. 63-68.

17. R. Bultmann in _Kerygma und Mythos_ II, p. 188.

18. _Ibid.,_ p. 192; see also _Jesus Christus und die Mythologie, op. cit.,_ p. 63.

19. _Ibid.,_ p. 192.

20. Not only in the case of Bultmann, who follows the "younger" Heidegger of _Sein und Zeit_ here, but also in the cases of E. Fuchs (in _Hermeneutik, op. cit.,_ and _Zur Frage nach dem historischen Jesus,_ Tübingen, 1960) and G. Ebeling (especially in _Theologie und Verkündigung,_ Hermeneutische Untersuchungen zur Theologie 1, Tübingen, 1963, and _Wort Gottes und Tradition,_ Göttingen, 1964), both of whom follow the "later" Heidegger (see _The Later Heidegger and Theology_ in New Frontiers in Theology, I, ed. by J. M. Robinson and J. B. Cobb, New York, 1963, and _The New Hermeneutic,_ New Frontiers in Theology, II, New York, 1964), I cannot rid myself of the impression that the philosopher himself (Heidegger) would be unable to recognize himself in this theological use of his earlier philosophy and the later philosophy which he developed from it. Going contrary to their own theme, but apparently on the basis of their faith (in concrete, Protestant Christianity), these theologians have "formalized" the philosopher's self-understanding and, in so doing, have neutralized its content and dissociated it from Heidegger's distinctively philosophical sphere of questioning. Both the idea of "existence" (Bultmann) and the idea of "being" (the putting into words of reality in Fuchs and Ebeling) have been formalized, in order that (or perhaps with the result that?) it may appear that their content (in the sense of personal choice or decision, _das Existenzielle_) is only given by the Christian relevation. These philosophers want above all to be authentically Christian. But in this way, they avoid the real problem that is situated in the tension between human self-understanding and understanding of the faith on the basis of the distinctively Protestant interpretation of the universally Christian principle of _sola gratia_ and replace this with a rather innocent problem—philosophy provides formal and neutral structures of existence and being, faith on the other hand provides the existential decisions about content. Faith thus becomes the overcoming of all metaphysics, even if this is set up existentially. H. M. Kuitert is right in saying, in _De realiteit van het geloof. Over de anti-metafysische tendens in de huidige theologische_

ontwikkeling, Kampen (1966), that the present-day crisis in faith is essentially a crisis of metaphysics, but he simply consents to it, and this apparently has its recoil in the Protestant question about how to deal with the Barthian "positivism of revelation." It is possible to ask oneself whether the Reformation is not consistently heading towards a destruction of all metaphysics, while the traditionally Catholic view of revelation is threatening to become silted up in *essentialist* metaphysics. Heidegger himself—see the quotation at the head of this article—has repeatedly warned us against a "Christian misuse" of his philosophy; see also *Über den Humanismus,* Frankfurt a. M., originally *Platons Lehre von der Wahrheit,* Berne (1947), especially pp. 21 and 35. But is not there a non-essentialist metaphysics?

21. The distinction between *existenzial* and *existenziell* goes back to Heidegger. The first ("existentialistic") self-understanding points to the descriptive analysis of "human existence" as such, whereas the second ("existential") self-understanding points to the personal and decisive encounter with reality. See *Sein und Zeit, op cit.,* p. 12.

22. R. Bultmann, among other places, *Glauben und Verstehen* I, pp. 161, 264 and 157 ff.; *Kerygma und Mythos* VI–1, pp. 24–26; *Kerygma und Mythos* pt. 2, p. 191 and *passim.*

23. H. Diem, *Dogmatik. Ihr Weg zwischen Historismus und Existenzialismus,* Munich (1955); *Der Irdische Jesus und der Christus des Glaubens* (Sammlung Gemeinverständlicher Vorträge 215), (1957).

24. L. Steiger, *Die Hermeneutik als dogmatisches Problem,* Gütersloh (1961). See also K. Schwarzwäller, *Theologie oder Phänomenologie?,* Munich (1966), although this author is less convincing and shows less understanding of "Bultmannism."

25. P. Ricoeur, *Existence et herméneutique, op. cit.,* in which the author correctly criticizes Heidegger for having taken "too short a route"—it is only from the applied hermeneutics of the diverse sciences that a philosophical and critical reflection about the conditions of understanding can be undertaken. See also *Histoire et vérité,* Paris (1955).

26. Denzinger, *Enchiridion Symbolorum,* ed. A. Schönmetzer, 1507 (786).

27. For the objectivity and meaning of historiography, see especially P. Ricoeur, *Histoire et vérité, op. cit.;* H. Marrou, *De la connaissance historique,* Paris ([4]1954), which was highly praised by Ricoeur, and partly accepted but strongly criticized by Rudolf Bultmann, at least in the German edition of *Geschichte und Eschatologie,* Tübingen (1958) which had previously appeared in English; R. Aron, *Dimensions de la conscience historique,* Paris (1961); P. Thévenaz, *L'homme et l'histoire,* Paris (n.d.); H.-G. Gadamer, *op. cit.;* L. Febvre, *Combats pour l'histoire,* Paris (1953); E. Betti, *Teoria*

generale della interpretazione, 2 parts, Milan (1955); P. A. Sorokin, *Social and Cultural Dynamics*, 4 parts, New York (1937–41); E. Castelli, *Les présupposés d'une théologie de l'histoire*, Paris (1952).

28. P. Ricoeur, *Existence et herméneutique, op. cit.*, p. 34.

29. M. Heidegger, *Unterwegs zur Sprache*, Pfullingen (1959), pp. 95–98.

30. H.-G. Gadamer, *Wahrheit und Methode, op. cit.*, pp. 483–84.

31. *Ibid.*, p. 484.

32. The meaning both of tradition and of "prejudgments" was, in Gadamer's opinion, devalued and unfavorably interpreted by the philosophers of the Enlightenment; see H.-G. Gadamer, *op. cit.*, pp. 255 ff.

33. G. Marcel, *Le déclin de la sagesse*, Paris (1954), pp. 43 ff.; see also E. Husserl, "Die Frage nach dem Ursprung der Geometrie als intentional-historisches Problem," *Revue Internationale de Philosophie* 1 (1939), pp. 203–26, especially pp. 207, 212 and 220.

34. H.-G. Gadamer, *op. cit.*, pp. 289–90.

35. J. B. Metz, *Christliche Anthropozentrik*, Munich (1962).

36. M. Heidegger, *Was heißt Denken?*, Tübingen (1954), p. 72; see also F. Wiplinger, *Wahrheit und Geschichtlichkeit*, Freiburg (1961).

37. H.-G. Gadamer, *op. cit.*, pp. 318–19. Thomas also provides valuable hermeneutical principles in his commentaries on Aristotle (especially in *In Peri hermeneias*). According to him, the living relationship to truth plays a fundamental part in the interpretation of a text in which truth is expressed. Gadamer who, like Fuchs and others, is inspired by the Greek philosophers, would have been able to find a great deal of hermeneutical material here (and in other commentaries by Thomas).

38. W. Pannenberg, "Hermeneutik und Universalgeschichte," *Zeitschrift für Theologie und Kirche* 60 (1963), pp. 101 ff., especially p. 116.

39. J. Moltmann, *Theologie der Hoffnung*, Munich (1965), especially pp. 250–79.

40. This has already been hesitantly affirmed by W. Kasper, *Dogma unter dem Wort Gottes*, Mainz (1965).

41. Gadamer, who was on the right track in seeing "juristical hermeneutics" in its "exemplary significance" for all hermeneutics (pp. 307–23), did not avail himself of this perspective so as to expose the very essence of the only hermeneutics with which a theologian can ultimately work—the hermeneutics of doing in faith, on the basis of God's promise. I am simply touching upon a perspective here which I hope to be able to develop elsewhere.

42. M. Heidegger, *Was ist Metaphysik?*, Frankfurt a. M. (⁷1955), p. 50.

43. All this implies that it is the believers themselves, as a confessing

community, who support the whole work of hermeneutics, because the subject of faith is not an "I," but a "we," and because the reinterpretative aspect belongs to the act of faith itself—obedience in faith, listening in faith to God's word, is, after all, also an *interpretation* in faith.

44. H.-G. Gadamer, *op. cit.*, p. 502.

45. See my article on this: "Ecclesia semper purificanda," *Ex auditu Verbi* (Theologische Opstellen aangeboden aan prof. C. Berkouwer), Kampen (1965), pp. 216–32.

II

Secularization and Christian Belief in God

It is clear that Christian revelation in its traditional form has ceased to provide any valid answer to the questions about God asked by the majority of people today, nor would it appear to be making any contribution to modern man's real understanding of himself in this world and in human history. It is evident that more and more people are becoming increasingly unhappy and dissatisfied with the traditional Christian answers to their questions. It is their questions about God himself which are involved above all, and there is unmistakable evidence of a growing desire everywhere for new answers to be given to new questions concerning him. The situation requires us to speak of God in a way quite *different* from the way in which we have spoken of him in the past. If we fail to do this, we ourselves shall perhaps still be able to experience God in outmoded forms, but clearly our own witness of and discussion of God will be met by most people with headshaking disbelief as mumbo-jumbo. It is partly because we are blind to the "signs of the times" that God's word, in all that we say of him, is returning to him void—just the opposite of what the Old Testament prophet assured us would happen.

The criticism of the traditional way of speaking of God which is now being voiced within the Christian churches, both Protestant and Catholic, arises, on the one hand, from the deepest values which these churches really aim to embody and, on the other hand, from the new, rational and secular sphere of understanding within which people are now seeking a meaning for human life.

In the biblical, patristic and medieval periods, man viewed and appraised everything directly in the light of the *causa prima et ultima,* the "first and last cause," following the Augustinian world-view. Medieval wisdom and science had little to offer him in the way of improving his life in this world, which was filled with the Church's ethical and explicitly religious values and the ultimate perspective of a happy existence hereafter. This was the real horizon of his life. The Church tried, of course, to alleviate misery in this world by works of charity, but man's intellect seemed not yet to have discovered its special task and its possibilities for the future.

Nonetheless, a glimpse was caught of man's technical ability to improve his lot on earth in the twelfth century, owing not to European discoveries but to chance encounters with the East during the Crusades. As a result, the twelfth century acclaimed the *ars mechanica* (technology) with as much enthusiasm as that which greeted the first launching of a satellite in our own time.[1] The water wheel, which could perform the work of many men and even of twenty-four horses, was (re-) discovered, and windmills, levers, the compass, the mechanical timepiece, and so on, all brought more humanity into the world, and the world became a rather more human place to live in. But it was not yet realized that an independent value was presenting itself here, and the fact that it resulted in a life more worthy of man has therefore to be accepted as coincidental.

At the same time, however, as man found out at once, technology could also be a source of new misery. All kinds of new and ingenious instruments of war were invented, instruments

which were condemned as early as 1139 at the Second Lateran
Council because of their murderous power. Then, as now, the
"rise of technology" was interpreted by some as the work of
the devil, claiming to improve on the work of God's creation.[2]
This view persisted obstinately, even into the reign of Philip II
of Spain. A suggestion was submitted to the country's ad-
ministrators for making the Rivers Tajo and Manzanares
navigable and thus create greater possibilities for certain isolated groups of the population. This was rejected by the gov-
ernment commission. They admitted that the situation in
which these people lived was unsatisfactory and indeed un-
tenable, but, "if God had so willed that these rivers should be
navigable," the commission said in its explicit vindication of
its disapproval of the plan, "then he would have made them
so with a single word, as he did formerly when he said 'fiat
lux' (let there be light). It would be a bold infringement of the
rights of Providence if human hands were to venture to try to
improve what God for unfathomable reasons has left unfin-
ished."[3] This historical event depicts in its most acute form a
basic characteristic of medieval and Augustinian man—his
acceptance of the static *status quo* of this world, the foundation
of which was God himself and the evils of which were ab-
sorbed as far as possible by works of charity. A rational understanding as the principle on which to base a plan for the future
within the world was beyond the range of medieval man—
with the exception of politicians who, despite everything that
the philosophers and theologians might say, were certainly
capable of manipulating human society.

As a result of the later development in the West of rationalization in the service of mankind, modern man began to discover the *world,* and thus *himself* as well, in an entirely new
way; that is, as a situated freedom which, through the col-

laboration of men, must give itself its own definite character in a task which gives meaning in this world, within a rational sphere of understanding, so that justice, peace and love may prevail among men. Man has now begun to plan *himself,* looking towards the future. Although it may or may not be explicitly formulated, it can scarcely be disputed that this is the new pattern of mankind's life today. But we must be critical in our attitude towards the possibility of its total *realization.* It is, after all, obviously marred by equally unmistakable abuses of freedom and ultimately also by the "sin of the world."

Secularization, which was the natural consequence of the discovery and the gradual widening of man's rational sphere of understanding, has in fact passed through a whole series of stages. I propose now to locate a few important turning-points in this development.

Secularization as the Consequence of the Discovery and the Progressive Widening of Man's Rational Sphere of Understanding

Four turning-points can be distinguished in the historical development of the Western process of secularization, at least in the area of theological and philosophical reflection. The theological and philosophical development cannot, after all, be considered as an autonomous growth within a closed sphere. On the contrary, it is embedded in socio-economic and political events. Therefore, if I speak of four turning-points in the secularization of the West, this will, of course, only be a bare outline. It will, moreover, be strictly limited to the level of reflection which, in turn, has to be seen against the background of a very complicated and living social reality. Nevertheless, it is precisely in reflection that this living reality achieves a more emphatic self-understanding. In its turn, this self-understanding influences and promotes the further process of development. Thus, these four turning-points seem to me to be extremely relevant to the process of secularization in the West.

(1) The deepest roots of secularization are, of course, to be found in our humanity itself, but it was in fact not until the twelfth and thirteenth centuries that the first signs of this secularization became clearly visible. At this time, a horizontal creatural network began to be built into the traditional Augustinian theology, which regarded man's relationship with God as an exclusively vertical one and to some extent as "extrinsic." This can be illustrated by two fundamental examples taken from many, the first at the ethical level and the second at the more general level of the theory of knowledge.

After a few sporadic attempts had been made by the scholastic theologians of the early Middle Ages, the thirteenth-century theologians began to insert a structure of the human *natura,* with its inherent "natural law" (*lex naturae*), in "between" God—with his "divine law" (*lex divina*) handed down by tradition of the Church and codified in the Bible and tradition—and man's *conscience*. This attempt had all the defects of any beginning. We must therefore be especially mindful of the intention that lay behind it and what it aimed to do. Its purpose was to humanize morality, to base it *in* man himself and thus to interiorize it, without denying its ultimately theist foundation.

The second example, which is much more fundamental, is to be found in the new attempt on the part of Albert and Thomas to build the horizontal structure of the *intellectus agens* "into" the medieval Augustinian doctrine of vertical "illumination." In this way, the principle of the legitimacy of a rational sphere of understanding—although it remained within the all-embracing understanding of faith—was established for the first time in the history of Christianity. In spite of its secularization, this new orientation remained within the one supernatural, Christian perspective. But it soon became apparent that the Church's attitude towards this phenomenon was to be a negative one. In 1277, the bishop of Paris, Etienne Tempier, condemned 217 propositions—an action which unmistakably foreshadowed the rather "reactionary" attitude which the Church was to take towards the process of secularization and the consequences of the acceptance of a rational sphere of understanding. Still, more and more historians are rightly coming to see the thirteenth century as fundamentally a century of laicizing rather than as a century of the cathedrals under whose towers this secularization took place. Initially, it was a *Christian* secularization, the protest made by the official Church notwithstanding.

(2) The last quarter of the sixteenth century marks the second turning-point. Apart from a few beginnings made round about the middle of the sixteenth century, especially by certain theologians of Louvain, a basic change in the history of the West occurred with Bellarmine, who was the first to teach with complete clarity the so-called theory of "pure nature" (*natura pura*),[4] which stated for the first time in history the principle that man has both a supernatural destiny and a destiny within this world. This meant a break not only with the patristic period and the Middle Ages, but also with the sacral world before and outside Christianity. It was the beginning of what may be called "horizontalism" (a misleading image, certainly, but a suggestive one). I am not implying that the *natura pura* theory was the active origin of the modern tendency towards secularization. Probably quite the reverse is the

case—the *natura pura* theory came about as an interpretation (albeit inadequate and basically unsuccessful) of a new understanding of man that had gradually arisen on almost all sides at that turning-point between the late Middle Ages and the early Renaissance when man was beginning to accept the full value and dignity of his being man within this world. The constitutive difference between this new sense of man and the world and the older biblical, patristic and scholastic view of life is most strikingly revealed in the new, and until then completely unknown, theological idea of the *natura pura;* that is to say, in the acceptance of the fact that being man—whatever this might mean in the concrete—was significant in itself, quite apart from any question of a supernatural destiny.[5] This new orientation remained traditional, however, in the sense that God was still thought to be within the rational sphere of understanding. A "natural theology" was thus maintained.

(3) However much the Reformation was a return to the biblical, patristic and medieval vision of the one religious and supernatural destiny of human life, it nevertheless—as the third turning-point in Western history—contributed in a radical way to further secularization, so much so that some historians and theologians have—incorrectly, I think—ascribed the process of secularization entirely to the Reformation. It was particularly by its denial of the traditional conviction that it was possible to speak about God in a meaningful way within the rational sphere of understanding that the Reformation really encouraged the advance of the process of secularization that had already begun. This interpretation, which the Catholics labeled "fideism," left the world, as world, in its full secularity. The reality of God now fell outside the rational sphere of understanding, which was, in the meantime, on its way towards controlling the concrete life of Western man.

Thus, the verticality of the newly flourishing spiritual life, the Christian witness of the Reformation, came to stand at right angles to the horizontal level of secular life in the world. Sooner or later, this was bound to produce Bultmannism and post-Bultmannism, notwithstanding the protests of Karl Barth.

(4) Via the Enlightenment, the *credere* of the Reformation took on the form of *intellegere* in Immanuel Kant, whose thought seems to me to be the fourth turning-point in the process of secularization. According to Kant, the objective reality of God could be neither proved nor refuted by "pure reason" (*reine Vernunft*). "God" was, for Kant, not a concept derived from empirical data but a "transcendental ideal." The division between religion and the rational sphere of understanding which had taken place with the Reformation was thus confirmed by Kant. The fact that he brought God within the context of morality and "practical reason" (*praktische Vernunft*) does not change this in any way; it was not to be long before the light of rational understanding penetrated here too and God was cast out. Schleiermacher was still able to locate an area of human life where rationality had not yet penetrated—that of the emotions and feelings, in which he saw the ground wherein religion could take root. But not long afterwards, feelings too were subjected to scientific analysis. The rational sphere of understanding became wider and wider and there seemed to be no place for God within its range.

Moreover, the empirical sciences acquired their philosophical foundation from Kant in the "analytical judgment" of pure reason. The natural sciences and the humanities and later what have come to be known as the gamma disciplines or behavioral sciences[6] could demonstrate their effective and fruitful contribution to the building up of the world into a place fit for man to live in. These above all represent the rational sphere of understanding within which man's life is planned towards a more human future.

This long process of secularization meant, in fact, that religion, the churches and theology suffered a functional loss. A new, independent world came into being alongside the Church. But the Church continued to live in her old world until she was forced to realize that hers was a totally different world from the one in which very many people now live. The cleavage between the Church and the world has thus given the impression that there are two different worlds—the *world of past memory,* the Church, and the *world of the future,* that of dynamic mankind living within an all-embracing rational sphere of understanding.

The confidence that men in need had previously placed in the Church was transferred, because of this functional loss, to the sciences, technology, politics, welfare work and so on—all of them activities and institutions realized within a rational sphere of understanding. The traditional way of speaking of God and to God thus became gradually more difficult. Specialists in the new sciences also began to concern themselves with the phenomenon of religion, a field in which previously only the theologian had been held to be competent. The psyche of religious man was scientifically interpreted by depth-psychologists—whose interpretation of faith and religion is, moreover, at its own relative level, quite legitimate. In the same way, sociologists also began to interpret religion. Thus modern man was confronted with a certain ambiguity in his thinking about faith and his practice of religion. Religion had become "suspect."

All this undermined the traditional way of speaking of and to God. Experience too seemed to confirm the growing doubt —diseases which no prayer or miracle had been able to cure

were cured by modern drugs, fields which had remained in-
fertile despite sprinkling with holy water were made fertile by
chemicals, and human needs were alleviated by various social
provisions and economic changes in the structure of society. In
view of all this, man ceased to speak of and to God in the way
which had previously been taken for granted. Necessity, the
"mother of invention," was rationally conceived and, as experience showed, this approach proved much more effective than
prayer in mitigating human needs. The unique "miracle"
which might happen to an isolated and privileged person became almost a blasphemy to many others (the majority!) who
had to go on living without miracles. The result is that man
today finds it more difficult than he did in the past not only to
talk *about* God, but also to talk *to* God. Many people who have
been brought up explicitly as Christians quietly leave the
Church, while those who still continue truly to believe experience great difficulties in speaking of and to God.

What is more, believers, living in a society which has become
increasingly pluralistic in its views of life, have made the initially disturbing discovery that those who do not believe are
neither more stupid than they are nor less virtuous. They have
found out too that Christians have specific faults and lack
understanding in specific respects and that a great deal of
injustice has often been perpetrated "in the name of God." All
this has meant that the very meaning of religion, of talking
about and to God and of appealing to him, has become obscured. What was once the core of Western Christianity has
now become unintelligible—and for many even intolerable.

This process, which is of course still going on, has now
reached a stage where the historical background against which
it took place has been forgotten and a new vocabulary is being
sought to define its present stage. Instead of talking about

secularization, sociologists are tending more and more to talk about "differentiation," and in France the theory of "structuralism" is gaining ground. But, whatever name we give to this child of modern thought—and he has a right to many names—we should not neglect the other side of this social process. Secularization is, after all, also an expression of man's fundamental uncertainty in a new world which he himself has designed. In the past, uncertainty and spiritual distress were the consequence of a *status quo* world upon which man seemed unable to have any effect. Now, however, it is precisely this self-made, more and more manipulated world which causes his anxiety. The process of rationalization and man's increasing ability to manipulate the world belong to the "instrumental" level—that is, to the level of the means and the less fundamental meanings of human life and not to the level of the *real* meaning of all this. Fear of the future hangs over secular mankind. All kinds of "spiritual movements" are emerging, and they are most in evidence where secularization has taken effect most completely. The progress of secularization has been accompanied by an increase in all kinds of neuroses and psychoses and of phenomena such as the consulting of horoscopes. In our welfare society, increasing rationality of the means clearly goes together with a loss of meaning and an obscuring of the ultimate values, thus with a decreasing rationality and a diminishing vision of the deeper, really meaningful human aims.[7] I in no sense mean to imply here that scientific and technical culture has been a *choice* on the part of the Western world, a choice of one from many other possibilities, one which could or might have turned out otherwise. I see this scientific and technical development as a necessary, essential part of human culture, in the last analysis part and parcel of humanity itself.[8] By loss of meaning and reality, I mean only

the lack of integration of this scientific and technical culture
into the *totally human* cultural task. Hominization is not yet
humanization. Precisely on the basis of this new situation, the
religious question has become relevant in a new way to our
society.

All this is what we have witnessed in the last few years. For
the most recent stage through which history is passing in this
whole scheme of social change is indeed concerned (apart
from many different forms of atheism) with a radical reinterpretation of religion itself, of Christianity and of the
Christian way of speaking of God. Without drawing any
sharp dividing lines, it is possible to distinguish two tendencies
in this reinterpretation—the first calls itself, paradoxically,
"Christian atheism," the second concerns the various *modified*
forms of this "death of God movement."[9] Both movements
take as their point of departure the radical identity between
the love of God and Christian human fellowship. The second
movement appears to be concerned with a real love of God,
but in the exclusive form of *devotio* or dedication to our
fellow-men. Of the first group, those who call themselves
Christian atheists, we may ask, not whether they are really
atheists, but whether they are not advocating a complete ab-
sorption of the love of God in love of our fellow-men—albeit
in the sign of the man Jesus as their living example—with the
result that the idea "love of God" no longer has any real meaning at all.

These tendencies have made the arguments of Dietrich
Bonhoeffer, who had already challenged us with his ideas of
a "secular interpretation of the Bible"[10] and "religionless
faith,"[11] even more forceful. Even Herbert Braun's explicit
affirmation that an existential interpretation of the Bible is
possible without reference to God[12] appeals to many people,

despite the protest raised by no less a person than Rudolf Bultmann, who appears unaware that it is not he himself but others who are drawing logical conclusions from his points of departure. Thus radical theology either pleads for a *definitive* silence about God (as do, for different reasons, Thomas Altizer, Herbert Braun and Paul van Buren, among others) or else calls for a provisional, *waiting* silence about God (as does William Hamilton, at least in his earlier essays). Christian faith therefore remains no more than concern for the building up of a world that is more worthy of man and for a fuller development of all peoples everywhere.

What is new about this experience is that it is apparently taken entirely for granted and is very widely spread over the whole world. The fact that it is rather a fashionable phenomenon undoubtedly plays an influential part in this, but a fashionable phenomenon is clearly not simply and solely all it is.[13] Men talk these days about a post-Christian stage of history, but they could just as well talk about a "post-Marxist" stage, since all the values that have been handed down to us in monologue are now being called into question. So it is that people everywhere are engaged in dialogue, searching for a fundamental reinterpretation of both Christianity and Marxism. Why else has dialogue become one of the most fashionable words of the twentieth century, if not because this century has witnessed the failure of all *systems* which were totalitarian in that they acknowledged only monologue? It is the failure of monologue which we are now experiencing—the Middle Ages were one great monologue; the Reformation and the Counter-Reformation were two parallel monologues; the Enlightenment was ultimately a secularization of the *rabies theologica*—the *écrasez l'autre* of the Crusades and the Inquisition became *écrasez l'infâme,* but it remained a monologue. And as the empirical sciences developed, they took over the dominant role from absolutist metaphysical thought. Always the black-and-white approach of monologue!

The twentieth century is experiencing the bankruptcy of all systems, including Christianity as a monological system. And so we are now all beginning a dialogue with each other. The truth is not to be found in a system, but in a dialogue, in a sphere that is common to all of us, because we have become aware that no one has a monopoly of the truth and that the truth transcends all our thoughts and yet lives among us. It is experienced not in the soloist's song, but in the polyphonic chorus of all mankind. You may know the story of the four blind men who met an elephant. They touched the animal. The first touched its feet and said, "This is a building with Doric columns." The second touched its trunk and said, "This is a snake." The third felt its belly and said, "This is the dried skin of a lion." The last man felt its ears and said, "This is a leaf of a palm tree." They began to argue and finally to fight for their truth which left no room for the other man's truth. This is a parable of the history of the Western world, at least as far as its darker side is concerned.

The question that now poses itself is this: Is the present situation leading to the end of Christianity? Or to the end of what could be called "conventional" or "traditional" Christianity?[14] And, if the latter is the case, is there not a danger that authentic as well as inauthentic aspects of Christianity will be lost? The problem narrows down to the question of how we, as men of faith in a secularized world, can still speak of God. A quick survey would seem to indicate that the most obvious interpretation of the Bible in our secularized world would be an *atheistic* one. Unintentionally, radical theology has at least made clear once again that faith in God is not something that can simply be taken for granted, but rather something that demands essentially a fundamental *metanoia,* a conversion. In a so-called Christian world, we cheapened Christian faith into a condition of healthy human understanding of the obvious. Modern thought has thrust before our faces the inconceivable wonder of faith's interpretation of reality, based on a fundamental *metanoia* in relation to the evident worldly experience of reality. We are reminded of the words of Tertullian: "Christians are made, not born."[15]

Before we go more deeply into the question of speaking of and to God in a secularized world, we should be more precise about what we mean by the term secularization, as the "endpoint" of the whole process. It seems to me that a distinction between two levels, that of the phenomenon itself and that of its interpretation, will help to clarify the problem. On the one hand, then, we must consider the process of secularization as a socio-cultural and historical phenomenon, in which the world and human society are conceived within the rational sphere of understanding. This level is, I think, fundamental. Compared with the past history of Western civilization, this implies that the world and human society have been withdrawn from the tutelage of the Church and religion. This results precisely in the positive secularity of the rational sphere of understanding, also including desacralization.[16] Man is planning a future for the world, and himself, which will be his own creation and, as a consequence of this, it cannot be denied that one of the sources which in fact nourished piety has disappeared. In the past, piety clearly drew much of its strength from man's impotence within the sphere of this world.

Secularization is therefore not simply a cultural phenomenon—it at the same time also implies, when seen from the point of view of religion, the distinction between the "God of

faith" and the "God of religion." A *"religionless* faith" is therefore, seen from the socio-cultural and historical point of view,
an implication of secularization, in which by "religion" (here
intentionally distinguished from "faith and divine worship")
is meant religious experience at a cultural stage of man's history when the rational sphere of understanding had not yet
been explicitly discovered in its full extent, with the result that
"faith and divine worship" took over those *functions* of this
world for which human ability was inadequate. "Faith and
divine worship" thus included a broad margin of "religion."
Hence the process of secularization seems to me to be fundamentally the discovery of man's rational sphere of understanding, a self-understanding of man which naturally takes
place in history, with the result that secularization is given
with the growth of humanity itself. In this respect, the process
of secularization is clearly a positive achievement.

On the other hand, however—and here we come to an entirely different level, that of the *interpretation* of this cultural
and sociological phenomenon—secularity is interpreted as atheism and is, furthermore, interpreted as such *because* many
think that faith in God remains an obstacle to secularization
in the socio-cultural and historical sense. In other words, the
idea of the "God of religion" is historically so heavy with the
customs of the past that for many people the end of the "God
of religion" is also the end of the "living God," the God of
faith. The cultural phenomenon—and secularity is this in the
first place—is therefore often presented together with this atheistic interpretation. The whole—both the phenomenon and its
interpretation—is thus called quite simply secularization, and
this word has consequently acquired an apparently inevitable
ambiguity. It should therefore be made clear that this "atheism" is an ideological interpretation and that the existing cul-

tural phenomenon which is interpreted in this way can be made intelligible without recourse to this atheistic interpretation—that it can be integrated in a way that is meaningful from the Christian point of view.

The Basis of our Silence about God and our Speaking of and to God

(1) What in the first place characterizes our new image of man and the world is that our old image of God has evaporated. We can no longer live by it because it is associated with our old image of man and the world. But even more characteristic is our apparent inability to form for ourselves a new image of God, an inability that is clearly reflected in the books and articles that have been written about the "death of God." In the past, Christian thinkers have always been clearly conscious of the fact that God was unapproachable, that he could not be described, and that man was fundamentally incapable of putting his knowledge of God into words or forming any adequate image of him. In the usual theology, spirituality and preaching of the past, however, God was often presented and experienced as someone who intervened in the world, and ideas of God derived from the qualities theologically predicated of him were too often manipulated as if they were adequate concepts of God. In all this man's religious experience continued to be authentic; yet it was contained within a social and culture context which colored man's inward religious experience then but has now been superseded.

Concepts such as "religionless faith" are therefore extremely ambiguous because they fail to make sufficient distinction between faith and its essential functioning within a social and cultural context. This does not mean that faith itself was less

authentic in the past than it is now in our new social and cultural situation. Why should we take on airs and claim that our
present age has authentic faith, when in fact all that is in
question is a different relationship between man and the
world? We often unconsciously make religious statements
when we should in fact be making statements about man and
society. Certain situations in the past which seemed to call for
a direct appeal for God's intervention if they were to be dealt
with seem now, on the basis of our present knowledge, to have
arisen from a lack of human knowledge, technique, and so on,
and to be capable of adjustment by human means. Was the
faith of the Fathers for this reason, given their circumstances,
any less authentic? Man's religious experience has always been
partly conditioned by social factors, just as it is for us today.
Man had no need to wait for authentic faith until the scientists
were ready with their conclusions! It is simply that in our
modern world, so transformed and conditioned by science, we
have reasons and incentives in the experience of religion which
are different from those of the past. In this way, the foreign
elements of "religion" have been eliminated from faith and
divine worship and so we can indeed speak of a genuine
history of the authenticity of Christian faith within the life of
religious mankind. The authenticity of the faith of Abraham,
the father of all faith, was different in quality from that of a
modern believer.

We are today more conscious, not only theoretically but also
in practice, of the fact that we have no real concepts of God and
that every concept of God that can be offered is in fact godless,
because it denies God's transcendence. Thus, as a reaction, the
concept of God threatens to become marginal, a void,[17] an abstract nothing. Even the concept of God as "the wholly Other"
is one-sided in that it makes God so high and remote that we

can no longer see what possible influence this stranger can have on our lives. For as long as history continues, every concept of God will be inadequate and will need to be superseded, even our present so-called "silence" about God.

(2) The attempt to make a meaningful distinction between the "God of religion" whom the process of secularization has killed and the *living* God or the "God of faith" seems to me to be impossible, in a secularized world, unless it can be shown that our secular experience of existence itself contains elements which inwardly *refer* to an absolute mystery. If this were not so, even this *secularity* itself would collapse, or else it would have to be given at least a substructure of ideologies which would sacrifice the human person to a better future and thus result not in humanization but in dehumanization. It seems to me that in a secularized world fideism inevitably leads to the death of faith in the living God—in other words, to *atheism,* whatever the form this may take. It is therefore notable that both Altizer and Hamilton, when all is said and done, are aware of the influence on their thought not only of Tillich —though their strongest inspiration comes from him—but also of Barth, for whom God was the wholly Other of whom we can know absolutely nothing within a rational sphere of understanding.

As the absolute reality, God by definition eludes direct experience. Because of this, a humanly meaningful faith in God is only possible within a rational sphere of understanding if our human reality *itself* contains a real reference to God, which is therefore part of our experience. The facile assertion that it is precisely this datum which no longer appeals to modern man and no longer corresponds to his understanding of himself can, in my opinion, only be called a pseudo-scientific slogan which elevates, in a very uncritical manner, certain emphases which perhaps—or rather, manifestly!—catch the eye now onto the level of a *ne varietur* of man. Because man is a being whose essence it is to exist by way of understanding and self-understanding, he can only speak meaningfully about God if this affirmation is inwardly connected with his understanding of himself. It is impossible to formulate any statement about God which does not at the same time say something meaningful about man himself, or any statement about man which does not say something meaningful about God. This means that as soon as the historicity of man's existential experience had been discovered in reflection, we realized that our language about God must grow and change with the development of our existential experience. If this did not happen, what we said about God would, viewed in the light of linguistic analysis, become irrelevant, meaningless and empty.

Because what we say about God, in preaching and teaching, still frequently makes use of categories derived from an existential experience which belongs to an earlier stage in man's development—when *that* kind of language about God was still meaningful and relevant—an impasse inevitably results, now that we are in a more developed stage of human experience and reflection: people no longer understand what we are talking about. If speaking of God really means that we are at the same time saying something meaningful about man, then talking about God in categories that belong to an earlier stage of man's experience simply cannot involve anything that is meaningful either about—or to—modern man. This kind of talk will appear to him to be completely irrelevant to his contemporary experience and even as contradicting his deepest existential desires. It is difficult to avoid giving the impression that being a believer involves accepting absurdities as true and maintaining an image of man and the world that cannot be regarded as valid in everyday life.

From one point of view, the present crisis in Protestant and Catholic theology seems to me to be the extreme consequence of the denial of every form of "natural theology," a result of the cleavage between human experience and Christian faith which can be summed up under the general heading of "fideism." If such a cleavage is taken as a point of departure, sooner or later the inevitable consequence must be the acceptance of the view that Christian faith is a useless superstructure built onto human reality. If, however, I once again advocate a "natural theology," it is not at all my intention to think of this in the traditional sense. In traditional natural theology, the problem was, after all, limited to the purely speculative level, and it was this which led to failure.

Therefore, confronted as we are now with atheism and with the so-called "Christian atheism" of the radical theologians, it seems to me to be less urgent to discuss directly the so-called proofs of the existence of God—the answer that believers give to the religious question—and more important to investigate the legitimacy of the question itself. Even from the hermeneutical point of view, this is the most important consideration—whether the question itself is justified. In personal conversations with American "death of God" theologians and with Dutch humanists it has become clear to me that even a so-called "meaningful" answer to a question that cannot be justified remains, of course, meaningless. They are certainly prepared to admire the consistency of a traditional or of a modern theistic analysis of man's existential experience and of the thematic answer to the quest for God, but they doubt the *legitimacy of the question itself*.

For this reason, what must, in the first place, be sought is what the linguistic analysts call the "disclosure"—the existential situation in which what can be directly experienced empirically discloses and evokes something deeper than that which is immediately experienced, something that reveals precisely the deeper basis and condition of possibility of the secular event.[18] What must be disclosed is the real basis of the "underground," existential trust in life that many people possess, not reflectively but nevertheless quite unmistakably, despite moments when absurdity forces itself on them—that fundamental trust that the future has meaning on the basis of the unspoken assumption that being man—the impossible—is nonetheless possible. This existential trust can be discovered, though only implicitly, even in the writings of those philosophers—like Albert Camus, for example—who describe human life as absurd. What must be investigated are the implications of the fact that there are people—whether believers or not—who have definitely opted for goodness and who therefore affirm that they regard human life as ultimately meaningful; people who, in spite of everything and above all in spite of man himself, refuse to be shaken in their conviction that it is not evil but goodness which has the last word. Is not this factual datum, which often presents itself before people have asked themselves the religious question, already a decision in favor of or against God; or rather, does it not ultimately justify the religious question, and the objective urgency of this question, because this trust cannot be justified when it is viewed only within the perspective of man himself taken as a whole?

It does seem to me that anyone who disregards this datum will be falling prey to an enormous historical naiveté. This manifest trust in life which many people have and the fact that others categorically deny it is a datum which I, as a believer, am bound to interpret in this sense: every man either accepts or denies that the fact of human existence is a *promise of salvation* which cannot be explained in the light of man's concrete being, and he makes this decision before he explicitly asks himself the religious question. Thus faith in God's unconditional love, in God as man's future, has already been either accepted or refused. The so-called proof of the existence of God which is based on the experience of contingency is therefore only the reflective justification, made afterwards, of the conviction that this unconditional trust in the gift of a meaningful human future is not an illusion, not a projection of frustrated wishful thinking, but that it has an objective basis in experienced reality—the reality in which the God who is to come manifests himself, and in a very intimate manner, as the one who is absent, but approaching nonetheless.

In this interpretation a basic criticism of the closed secular character of the "Christian atheism" of radical theology is implied, but at the same time one of the latter's deepest insights is given its true value. It has, after all, become clear that nowadays it is scarcely possible to maintain that a *reflective* "natural knowledge of God" is indispensable to the understanding of Christianity; in our time Christianity—and indeed an intelligible, relevant and explicit Christianity—arises from quite different preconceptions and experience, namely, a radical commitment to the world by concern for our fellowmen, the struggle against evil and injustice in all its forms. The Christian sees in this the expression, as yet unthematized but nevertheless authentic, of a whole attitude which includes an element that he has come to recognize as the "natural knowledge of God," the condition which makes the venture of his Christian faith and unconditional surrender humanly intelligible.

A decisive question, then, is whether, in authentic self-transcendence, the attitude of fundamental trust in reality in spite of all experiences to the contrary is or is not present.[19] In the history of Christianity the reflective expression of this attitude is an explicit acceptance of God—the resurrection of the man Jesus, then, reveals itself as the real basis of this trust in life against all odds. Opening to reality in self-transcendence towards God is therefore the ontological condition which makes it possible for our minds to grasp the gratuitous revelation of salvation in Christ and at the same time it is a personal justification of the life of faith. As far as secularity itself is concerned, acceptance of God makes secularization meaningful without giving it an ideological substructure or degrading the human person as no more than a means of ensuring a better future. "Christian secularity" prevents the secularized world from imposing a modern form of "slavery" on man, a system in which the human person is sacrificed to an ideology or to the bringing about of a better world.

It constantly surprises me that Christians are still able to ask about *the extent* to which a Christian life includes commitment to the task of improving the world and to militant opposition to war, racial discrimination and all forms of injustice. On analysis, the acceptance of God is, in a different language game, the formulation of what is really involved in the realization of goodness in the world and the overcoming of evil. Acceptance of God is the ultimate, precise name which must be given to the deepest meaning of commitment to this world. If the matter is put in this way, the question as to whether and to what extent faith in God is really a stimulus to commitment to this world becomes incomprehensible. The real believer has already left this dilemma behind him. The building up of the world into a community of persons in justice and love appears on closer reflection—or, more precisely, in a "disclosure situation"—to coincide with acceptance of God and, in the concrete, even with faith in God. To refuse to give a place to evil in one's own life and in that of society and to combat it wherever it occurs is to give expression to one's trust that good must have the last word.

Not to lose faith in man in all his activities, despite all evil experiences, reveals itself, on closer analysis, as a latent, unconditional trust in God, as faith that human existence is a promise of salvation. It is already a first answer to the word that reality addresses to us—that we have been called into existence by an absolute Goodness. This is demonstrated in mankind's never ending attempt definitively to overcome evil and even death. But it is only in faith, from the life, death and resurrection of Jesus Christ that we learn that being man—the impossible—is nonetheless possible. God's act of creation, which we experience distinctly or indistinctly in man's trust in life, is a commitment to the task of militantly opposing all forms of injustice and at the same time the basis of the trust that the future is man's task: Jesus' life, death and resurrection is the divine promise that the future can and *will* be realized in and through our commitment in faith, despite all failure. Faith in the resurrection would, however, be an irrational leap (and anyone not venturing to take this "leap" would be just as right or even more right) if surrender in faith were not a truly *human* act. Within faith, then, it must be possible to indicate a rational way through our secular experiences towards God, a way which, in itself, does not lead to salvation, but which does make faith in the salvation that God extends to us in Jesus a mature and humanly meaningful act.

The fact that, contrary to all the indications provided by history, being man as a gift to the other is a meaningful possibility is expressed in the Bible with the words that the grace of the kingdom of God appears in the world of men—a kingdom of justice, love and peace, a kingdom in which there will be no more evil or misery and every tear will be wiped away (see 2 Pet. 3.13; Apoc. 21.4). Christian hope knows that this possibility has indeed been given to man as grace. The Christian thus lives in the consciousness of faith that his commitment here and now to the setting in order of temporal society is *not in vain.* He is, of course, not able to see how this setting in order of temporal society—which has clearly not yet become the eschatological kingdom itself—may at the same time be the commencement in obscurity of the *eschaton.* But hope in the radically new eschatological kingdom stimulates him never to be content when he has already achieved a victory in this world, since we shall never be able to say, historically, *this* is the promised future. In the Bible, the one who did say that was called the Antichrist. Christianity essentially implies living "post-terrestrially."

Commitment to this world, experienced as *faith,* thus forms an essential part of the Christian faith in God. But—and this is the vitally important complement—it is in and through our *active* trust in faith that *God's gift* is realized in history. On the one hand, it is possible to say that the Church, as the community of believers, (1) *participates* in God's activity in this world through her active hope, (2) "articulates" this activity of God, that is, gives it a *name,* as a testimony to the whole of the world, (3) proclaims the unconscious hope of the world and (4) must play a leading part in humanizing the world, must be in the vanguard in caring for man. On the other hand, however, it must be stated that the Church cannot carry out these functions and this mission if she does not also lead her *own* life, the distinctive life of the Church which nourishes these functions; in other words, if she does not celebrate in gratitude that from which this world may live—the reality of Jesus Christ, the Lord, the absolute and gratuitous presence of the living God.

Faith in God essentially implies an interpersonal relationship, a knowledge in faith of an absolute, personal "Opposite" with whom dialogue is possible. God, as a mystery, has been *directly* given to us to experience in the revelation in grace of God which is the Christian life of faith, even though this can only be indirectly expressed and conceptualized. Our experience of God is therefore always an interpretation and a making of human history in this world. But in religion we are concerned with *Someone,* and not simply with man and his history. And it is precisely this reality which is visibly expressed and proclaimed in the Church's liturgy of the Word and her Sacrament. If the Church becomes identical with "the world" and "improving the world" and means nothing more than this, she has already ceased to bring a message to the world. She has nothing more to say to the world and can only echo what the world discovered long since. I know from experience that it is precisely this which causes disillusionment in the "modern" Church among many lay people who are experts in the secular sphere—they have the impression that their Church—in other words, the faithful and some theologians—simply echoes what they were saying on the basis of scientific analysis ten or twenty years ago. In this way, the Church loses her relevance for the world. The so-called end of "conventional Christianity" is simply the end of Christianity itself. We may well ask whether *the faithful* are themselves not sometimes the cause of this fatal disillusionment in the Church.

If the Church has no message *of her own* to bring, a promise which the world cannot articulate for us, then she indeed has no further reason for existing. Only a Church which shows a face of her own and can give a name of her own to solicitude for our fellow-men in this world, and which can explain, proclaim and commemorate in celebration the personal and definitive meaning of this, still has something to say to a secularized world, and if she does this, she will also have her finest opportunities in a secular world. If the Church cannot make this message of her own a reality, the secularized world will be the scene of the most bizarre and irrational ventures—horoscopes, astrology and all kinds of sectarian movements will offer compensatory activities for life in the "secular city" of the "metropolis." But it is only the Church's own message, her faith in God's unconditional love of man, that can give a distinctive and meaningful consistency to secularity itself, without any ideological substructure or suprastructure.

Included in this, however, is the irreplaceable meaningfulness of personally and communally *dwelling upon* the personal mystery, since it is only within this personal mystery that human life in the world becomes ultimately and definitively meaningful as *personal* life in a *community,* and it is to this personal mystery that man knows himself to be ultimately responsible in his work in the world. The believer knows himself to be responsible, not only when confronted with the judgment and the memory of history, but also when confronted with the judgment of the living God. If God is not an infrapersonal being, a vague "substratum" or mystical and cosmic primordial ground of our existence, but a truly "living" God —and this is, after all our demythologization, still the essence of the biblical revelation—then Christianity also implies an *explicit attention* to the personal "Opposite," an attention which we can, moreover, only express relevantly in secular forms. Prayer and life in this world are therefore, for the believer, constantly flowing over into each other. *In* the world, he is nonetheless *with* God; and praying, dwelling upon God, he is nonetheless "with the world"; for, if this were not so, he would not be able to grasp God in his mind. It is only the focus of his attention that is always changing. In this, man in his prayer will never succeed in simply directing his attention towards God—God's nearness manifests itself only, as the mystics correctly say, in "the experience of a wall." Praying, the believer comes up against a blind wall, and anyone whose experience differs from this may speak as ardently as he likes about his experience of prayer, but it is hardly possible to say anything to him but that he does not know what prayer is and is deceiving himself. The experience of God is one which cannot, so to speak, be "isolated." The believer knows that God is present, but he experiences this presence only in the painful experience of "absence," which nonetheless betrays a very intimate nearness and thus keeps hope alive. Because God is transcendence? Yes, but even more precisely because, for someone who lives in time, God's transcendence is not only memory and not only, here and now, painfully experienced "absence," he is also the God who is to come, who goes ahead of us towards a future. We must therefore always be on the way in history and *make* history in order to be able to find him. Encountering God himself is an event that we shall not experience until the eschatological hour, but it is this which is being prepared for in man's history on this earth, a history which is, however, more than simply preparation—it is itself the *coming* of God, the transcendent one.

Prayer, the liturgy, the life of the Church as a whole, are extremely meaningful and, for a Christian, indispensable. But we should not forget that *they* refer us to the events of this world as the context in which God comes to us. Even if we take into account the strongly hellenized form of the Church's mystical tradition, this still remains a living witness to the fact that God can never be approached in isolation or by himself but that the genuine life of faith nonetheless remains magnetized by a prayerful longing for encounter with God. This is a stimulus which, on the one hand, radicalizes our commitment to this world and, on the other, prevents us from regarding this as the absolute point of rest. Being fully human is attained only in self-transcendence, and in the sense that what is more than human is involved, through the gift of God. In the gift the Giver, above all, continues to speak to our hearts. When one is given a bouquet, it is lovely in itself and a gift that warms the heart; but the real warmth, the response that one feels inwardly, has its origin in the giver himself. Human fellowship, or community between persons, finds its ultimate inward and definitive meaning only through community with an absolute "other Person": *that,* in the last analysis, proves to be the meaning of faith in God in a secularized world.

Summarizing all that I have said, it is possible to state that "faith in and worship of God," as opposed to "religion," cannot be defined as an *exclusive* relationship with God. It can only be defined as a specific way, which transcends itself, of approaching the totality of reality and of helping to realize this totality in God's active presence which, because it consists in absolute immediacy, is never subject to our will. This is unmistakably the authentic aspect that can be distilled from the new way of speaking about God in our own times—a way of *silence* which *allows* God to find expression in our concern and our work for the welfare of our fellow-men.

But silence is also a form of speaking. *Simply* being silent about God can therefore produce an even more fatal impasse than the one brought about by our limping speech about God, who in any case transcends everything we can say. To be silent about God, merely allowing him to be present as the "transcendent third" in our human relationships and our work for the world, speaks louder than words in declaring irrelevant that which is most important in life—the living source of our hope. It is precisely this that Paul denounced as man's idle "boasting." But in the community of men it is the inexpressible which must be loudly expressed—humanity itself expects this. Only the inexpressible is really worth discussing—it refreshes and kindles the mind. People are reduced to talking about such obvious things as the weather when they really have nothing to say.

The place where what is really relevant to man and ultimately inexpressible can be brought to expression should be precisely the Church. She would then serve as humanity's representative, an interpreter for the whole of mankind, the prophetess who gives a name to the mystery from which all men are to live. This proclamation by the Church then becomes a direct appeal and an invitation to those who, even in the light of the deepest mystery that inspires them too, seem to feel no need to formulate the reasons for their commitment to their fellow-men in this world.

It is, of course, understandable that not everybody feels this need. Some married couples, for example, who certainly experience a deep personal community in their daily cares, similarly have no need to talk about their love explicitly—this does not mean that love is lacking in their relationship and that they do not live from and for each other. But if the prose of life never flowed over into poetry, there would undoubtedly be a fatal void in the relationship, since this overflow is an essential element in day-to-day life. May we not therefore regard the Church as the one to whom Christ has given the task, perhaps as mankind's representative, of bearing witness to, expressing,

proclaiming and commemorating in grateful celebration the
inexpressible mystery from which this world may live, unconsciously, thanks to Christ's life, death and resurrection?[20]
Is the Church—and here I am deliberately putting out of mind
the pain of her failure and mine—not the poetry in the prose
of our lives? This does not mean that the Church is in any
sense distinct from the world, but equally she is not identified
with the world—she is the "*sacrament* of the world," the human community of believers which gives utterance to God and
proclaims him in the secular world, thanks him in Christ Jesus
and can say quite openly, in the name of all mankind: "God·
is my song." And it is precisely this which is the first humanizing task of the Church—to celebrate, to thank, and to commemorate, and in this way to engage in a relationship with
reality. Hence she could not be identical with the prosaic,
technical, secularized world, but she nevertheless sings her
song in the world and for the world's welfare.

So far no balanced solution has in fact been found in contemporary theology for the problem involved in reconciling
the concepts of "revelation" (according to, say, the one-sided
but authentic inspiration of Thomas Aquinas and Karl Barth,
or "orthodoxy") and "man's understanding of himself" (according to, for instance, the equally one-sided but also equally
authentic inspiration of Bultmannism, or the "bold reinterpretation of faith"). The reason for this seems to me to be the
fundamental ambivalence of the source from which modern
theology has found refreshment, "existential phenomenology."
Existential phenomenology is clearly declining in prestige in
the world of philosophy at the present time. Certain movements, not yet very clearly defined but manifestly anti-existen-
tialist in character, are bringing existential phenomenology,
hitherto predominant in the philosophy of our times, under

extremely heavy fire—e.g., French structuralism, the trend inspired by Ernst Bloch's "principle of hope" and the theology of history of the Pannenberg circle. But above all, perhaps, there is a tendency everywhere evident—discernible even in the work of a man like Paul Ricoeur, otherwise sympathetic towards existential phenomenology—to transcend the anti-Hegelian sentiment of existential phenomenology and try to establish a link with Hegel's set of problems and themes. The findings of phenomenological thought, which can no longer be disregarded, are of course not denied or minimalized by these movements, but its latent ambiguity is manifesting itself increasingly, as well as the effects of this ambiguity in the influence it has exerted on the existential interpretation of the Bible made by Bultmann and the post-Bultmann school. Phenomenological thought bears witness, on the one hand, to the "crisis of objectivity" and, on the other, to the "insufficiency of subjectivity." The fact that the distinctive manner in which existential phenomenology has tried to resolve the problem of object and subject is unsatisfactory is clearly echoed in present-day Protestant thinking and, stemming from this, in modern Catholic thought as well. An attempt is being made to solve the problem of discussing God without reverting, on the one hand, to the "objectivizing orthodoxy" and, on the other, to the nineteenth-century "liberalism of subjectivity." But it has not yet been possible to find a satisfactory balance between these two extremes.

It would seem as though Merleau-Ponty was aware, in the light of his phenomenological thought, of something of this kind, since he wrote, in *Sens et non-sens*,[21] that the Christian faith or the discussion of God could not be sustained except on a Thomist basis (in this, he was referring to objective orthodoxy in general—he could equally well have said on a Barthian basis); or unless, he added, Christianity perhaps developed into a faith without dogma, a believing openness without content. It seems to me that there is no longer any question that this tendency is noticeable in the thinking of Bultmann and his school and that, on the basis of existential phenomenological principles, the "death of God" theology and "Christian atheism" are its penultimate consequences (that is, Christian faith without any kind of reference to God). Theology, then, has been handed existential phenomenology's unpaid bill, and this bill is, above all, for the ambiguity that has continued to exist in connection with that philosophy's so-called solution of the problem of object and subject.

It is clear that objectivity and subjectivity are as much of a problem today as they were before the emergence of existential phenomenology. Present-day theology, both conservative and progressive, will only render the problem of faith more acute if it does not devote itself first of all to a serious search for a real hermeneutics of history which analyzes the ontological conditions making possible the retention of an authentic identity of faith *within* the reinterpretation of faith, a reinterpretation which in its turn is necessary because of man's situation in history. For we may well ask ourselves whether the modern reinterpretation of the faith and the revision of our way of speaking about God will really help Christianity to pass intact through its present unmistakable crisis. At the same time, however, we can question whether a theology which seeks its salvation in simply repeating the earlier statements about the faith literally is not equally posing a risk to "orthodox" faith, even if it is only by default; for in its ignorance of the hermeneutical bases of faith and inability to grasp their implications it is inevitably promoting the loss of faith, both by those who are silent and those who cry out in protest. Anyone who eliminates intellectual reinterpreting reflection from his faith is in fact declaring that there is a sphere in his life which is wholly un-connected with his faith—the sphere of the intellect. If such a person holds onto his faith, it stands to reason that he can do so only by behaving schizophrenically in a secularized world —leading a double life and adhering to a twofold truth. In reaction, either "Christian atheism" or a short-sighted "defense of the faith" will manifest itself. Both undermine genuine orthodoxy.

But let me close, as a believer, on a more hopeful, yet realis-tic note, with a *cri de coeur* from the first chapter of *Eclipse of God,* written by Martin Buber, the philosopher who was so much inspired by the Old Testament:

"Yes," I said, "it is the most heavy-laden of all human words. None has become so soiled, so mutilated. Just for this reason I may not abandon it. Generations of men have laid the burden of their anxious lives upon this word and weighed it to the ground; it lies in the dust and bears their whole burden. The races of man with their religious factions have torn the word to pieces; they have killed for it and died for it, and it bears their finger-marks and their blood. Where might I find a word like it to describe the highest! If I took the purest, most spar-kling concept from the inner treasure-chamber of the philoso-phers, I could only capture thereby an unbinding product of thought. I could not capture the presence of Him whom the generations of men have honored and degraded with their awesome living and dying. I do indeed mean Him whom the hell-tormented and heaven-storming generations of men mean. Certainly, they draw caricatures and write 'God' underneath; they murder one another and say 'in God's name.' But when all madness and delusion fall to dust, when they stand over against Him in the loneliest darkness and no longer say 'He,

He' but rather sigh 'Thou,' shout 'Thou,' all of them the one word, and when they then add 'God,' is it not the real God whom they all implore, the One Living God, the God of the children man? Is it not He who *hears* them? And just for this reason is not the word 'God,' the word of appeal, the word which has become a *name,* consecrated in all human tongues for all times? We must esteem those who interdict it because they rebel against the injustice and wrong which are so readily referred to 'God' for authorization. But we may not give it up. How understandable it is that some suggest we should remain silent about the 'last things' for a time in order that the misused words may be redeemed! But they are not to be redeemed *thus.* We cannot cleanse the word 'God' and we cannot make it whole; but, defiled and mutilated as it is, we can raise is from the ground and set it over an hour of great care."[22]

Notes

1. See L. Mumford, *Technics and Civilization,* New York (1963); J. de Goff, *La civilisation de l'Occident médiéval,* Paris (1964), chapter 7, pp. 249–318; M. Chenu, "Arts mécaniques et oeuvres serviles," *Revue des Sciences philosophiques et théologiques* 29 (1940), pp. 313–15 (reprinted in *La théologie au douzième siècle,* Paris, 1957, pp. 19–51).

2. *Ars mechanica* was traced back, by an etymological trick, to the root *moechia*—technology was a violation of human dignity. See P. Delhaye, *La microcosmos de Godefroid de S. Victor,* Lille (1951), p. 115; M. Chenu, "Arts mécaniques," *op. cit.,* pp. 313–15.

3. Quoted by M. Landmann in *Problematik, Nichtwissen und Wissensverlangen im philosophischen Bewußtsein,* Göttingen (1949), p. 55, note 13.

4. In his *Surnaturel,* Paris (1946) H. de Lubac wrongly attributed the *natura pura* theory to Cajetan, as did J. H. Walgrave in *Geloof en theologie in de crisis,* Kasterlee (1967). This statement was rightly attacked by H. Rondet in "Le problème de la nature pure et la theologie du XVIe siècle," *Recherches de Science Religieuse* 35 (1948), pp. 481–522, and by P. Smulders in "De oorsprong van de theorie de zuivere natuur," *Bijdragen* 10 (1949), pp. 105–27. De Lubac made a retraction of his earlier opinion in his later

book, *Augustinisme et théologie moderne,* Paris (1965), p. 188. Cajetan certainly anticipated a different feeling for life in his minimalist interpretation of the natural longing for grace, but it was Bellarmine who, after the way had been prepared by the Louvain theologians, R. Tapper and J. Driedo, and by Bañez, developed the *natura pura* theory.

5. It is quite true that the emergence of the *natura pura* theory can be attributed to speculation in the sixteenth century about the gratuitous character of grace, but the belief that this theory was necessary to confirm the gratuity of grace certainly originated in the context of the Renaissance. Basically, then, Baianism was a reaction against this novelty in the idea of *natura pura* and it must be judged in this light. The rehabilitation of Baius and Jansenius is the great merit of J. H. Walgrave's work cited above.

6. In the Netherlands, the humanities are called the alpha disciplines, the natural sciences are known as the beta disciplines, and the behavioral sciences are termed the gamma disciplines.

7. P. Ricoeur, "Tâches de l'éducateur politique," *Esprit* 33 (1965), no. 340, pp. 78–93; L. Newbigin, *Honest Religion for Secular Man,* London (1966), especially pp. 31 and 34; M. Heidegger, *Die Technik und die Kehre,* Pfullingen (1962); W. Weischedel, *Wirklichkeit und Wirklichkeiten,* Berlin (1960).

8. A. van Melsen, *Natuurwetenschap en ethiek,* Antwerp (1967), pp. 180–81.

9. T. Altizer and W. Hamilton, *Radical Theology and the Death of God,* New York (1966); T. Altizer, *The Gospel of Christian Atheism,* Philadelphia (1966). Representatives of the modified form of the "death of God movement" include H. Cox, *The Secular City,* New York (1966) and *God's Revolution and Man's Responsibility,* Valley Forge (1965); G. Vahanian, *The Death of God,* New York (1961) and *No Other God,* New York (1966).

10. D. Bonhoeffer, *Widerstand und Ergebung,* Munich (1961), *passim* (= *Letters and Papers from Prison,* London, 1967, *Prisoner for God,* New York, 1957). See also G. Ebeling, "Die nichtreligiöse Interpretation biblischer Begriffe," *Zeitschrift für Theologie und Kirche* 52 (1955), pp. 296–360.

11. D. Bonhoeffer, *op. cit.,* especially pp. 178 ff. See also H. Zahrnt, *Die Sache mit Gott,* Munich (1967) pp. 170–78 and 196–214.

12. H. Braun, *Gesammelte Studien zum Neuen Testament und seiner Umwelt,* Tübingen (1962), pp. 243–309, especially p. 297. On the basis of a narrowly empirical and somewhat obsolete linguistic analysis, Paul van Buren also makes the same affirmation in *The Secular Meaning of the Gospel,* London and New York (1963).

13. In other civilizations too, a process of secularization is taking place in

the present, and similar phenomena have even occurred in the distant past. It is possible, for example, to regard the philosophy of ancient Greece as a demythologizing interpretation of the gods of Olympus, and Titus Lucretius Carus, the Epicurean, wrote things in his *De rerum naturae* (published in Zürich in 1956; see also G. Hasenhüttl, *Der unbekannte Gott,* Tübingen, 1964) from which whole pages could be quoted and the modern reader would, if the author's name were withheld, think that they had been penned by such people as Harvey Cox, William Hamilton or Thomas Altizer, or even Karl Marx or Roger Garaudy.

14. W. van de Pol, *Het einde van het conventionele christendom,* Roermond and Maaseik (1966); see also the same author's *Op weg naar een verantwoord Godsgeloof,* Roermond and Maaseik (1967).

15. Tertullian, *Apologeticum* 18, 4 (*Corp. Christ. Lat.* I, 118): "Fiunt, non nascuntur christiani."

16. This secondary character especially (of an event with an essentially positive meaning) has been historically analyzed by H. Lübbe in his *Säkularisierung. Geschichte eines ideenpolitischen Begriffs,* Freiburg and Munich (1965). It should be borne in mind here that this secondary aspect may have acted as a stimulus to distinguish the essential aspect.

17. See C. Verhoeven, *Rondom de Leegte,* Utrecht (1966), p. 163.

18. See, among others, Schubert Ogden, *The Reality of God and Other Essays,* London (1967), pp. 1–70.

19. An analysis of death as man's complete gift of himself "in hope" is essential to a consideration of this problem, but I cannot discuss this in detail here.

20. This "representation" does not make the Church's mission any less urgent, but it gives it a different character.

21. Paris (1948), pp. 149 and 151.

22. Martin Buber, *Eclipse of God,* New York (Harper Torchbook), 1957, pp. 7–9.

III

Secular Worship and Church Liturgy

Doubts about the Meaning of Church Liturgy

William Hamilton says: "I do not see how preaching, worship, prayer, ordination, the sacraments can be taken seriously by the radical theologian."[1] This radical movement of the Church towards the world has already turned its back on such theologians as Rudolf Bultmann (whom it regards as conservative) and the whole of the post-Bultmann school, and has even disposed of Harvey Cox, who makes such a furore in certain circles, with the pleasant insinuation of neo-orthodoxy—"The Secular City (pop Barth)."[2] Even the Bishop of Woolwich, John A. T. Robinson, the author of *Honest to God,* is regarded as "behind the times."[3] This movement is not an expression of something that has been thought out by scholars in their studies and found its way across the world by means of translations. In my opinion, the very opposite is nearer to the truth. What many believers have experienced in their own lives since 1945, whether they have liked it or not, has simply been formulated and expressed systematically by these "Christian atheists" or, as they prefer to call themselves, "radical theologians." The Episcopalian Paul van Buren has now said quite openly—and thus more candidly than in his book—not only that theist ideas have been finally discarded but that the living God of the Bible has simply ceased to count, and that he, a clergyman, has not prayed for a long time and avoids liturgical services.[4] This is

93

a frank expression of what I too have often heard in Catholic
student circles, both clerical and lay, although I cannot really
say how high the percentage is among Catholics. In any case,
the phenomenon is a very real one. We must, of course, take a
certain tendency to follow fashion partly into account, especially now that so many of such books (in which many readers
recognize themselves) are available to all in cheap, easily ac-
cessible editions. But, however much this phenomenon may be
influenced by fashion, our daily experiences prove beyond all
doubt that "Christian atheism" is making giant strides throughout the world. Most young people, laymen and laywomen, who
enrol as students in the theological faculty at a university have
already read all the available books and articles in this field.
The very fact that a surprisingly large number does enrol in
such courses is proof of the intense interest in these intriguing
aspects of the religious problem of life.

In such a climate, those who are engaged in renewing the
liturgy are, of course, faced with serious problems. Liturgical
worship itself is already becoming a basic problem for many
people.[5] On the one hand, many older believers are shocked
and upset by liturgical renewals, whereas many of the younger
ones regard the entire liturgy, both in its older and in its renewed form, as already out-of-date—they have no further need
for it. It is, of course, true that this was said centuries ago,
during the Enlightenment, and the Church's liturgy has sur-
vived this rejection for more than a century and a half, but
pointing out how relative such manifestations are in the perspective of history will not make much impression on those
who support the new slogans. Christians could react by saying,
Very well, we will write these people off as Christians and go
over to the Church's order of the day! I believe, however, that
it is not, in our present time, up to Christians themselves to

determine the moment when the dialogue should be broken off. If it is broken off, then this should be done from outside. The believer himself should not take the initiative by threatening anathema. At least, I do not think that anything would be gained by it. But if the dialogue is broken off from outside, then all that remains for a Christian—averse to a ghetto Church, but certainly prepared to regard a diaspora Church as a real possibility for the future—is to bear witness, confess what Jesus, the Christ (all he has left), means for him and proclaim that the glorification of God's name *is, for him,* still the deepest meaning of his human life. He will, then, leave it to the future to judge who has most profoundly and most purely approached the relevance of human life and who has done most justice to man.

Nonetheless, Christians themselves, as believers in God, must put their convictions into practice in their own period, and for this reason they must listen to what H. Ringeling has called the "foreign prophecy" which appeals to us from the secularized world. Existential problems are rightly subjected to the criticism of Christianity, but in the same way Christian forms of life are subject to criticism in the light of new existential experiences. In the concrete, this latter criticism is directed towards a Christian life more or less identified with a "practice" of the faith in which liturgical worship runs parallel to a life which is fully immersed in the world. Any liturgical renewal which ignores this criticism will at the same time be ignoring the *kairos,* God's offer of grace here and now, and thus grace itself.

It is instructive to consider a passage taken from Paul Tillich's writings in connection with a text taken from one of the pronouncements made by the Second Vatican Council. In comparison with the new radical trend, both of these texts are "classical" theology and are therefore stigmatized as "out-of-date" by the radical theologians. The passage from Tillich is: "The existence of religion as a special realm is the most conspicuous proof of man's fallen state."[6] The conciliar text is: "They err no less . . . who believe that they can plunge themselves into secular concerns, as though these had nothing to do with the religious life, because they think that religious life consists only of acts of worship and of fulfilling certain moral obligations. This discrepancy between the faith that they confess and their everyday life must be regarded as one of the more serious errors of our times."[7] Both Tillich and the council are saying that, from the Christian point of view, the cleavage between worldly activity and liturgical worship is a disaster, and that this gap must be bridged. But then we are faced with the question, how? Should we regard secular life as worship and separate worship as meaningless? Or should liturgical worship be secularized and placed in the sphere of secular life with its terrestrial projects? Or does the worship of God which is practised in and through our worldly activity with our fellow-men of its very nature still demand a grateful celebration in the Church's liturgy? For, even if one denies that there is a dilemma between service to mankind and the glorifying of God's name—"God's glory is living man" (Irenaeus)—this Christian commitment to producing a world fit for all men to live in still confronts us with the problem of whether this directly useful service of our fellow-men does not call for the glorifying of God's name in an act that is not directly useful to the world—in other words, in the Church's liturgy. Anthropologically speaking, the question is this: Is *human life* meaningful without thanks-giving celebrations? We may well ask ourselves, with Gabriel Marcel, whether the disappearance of gratitude from the world is not a "falling off in wisdom."[8]

It is therefore not a question of trying to find *some* place in the world where man is failing constitutively to give meaning to the world and thus, in spite of everything, is still thrown back on God in order to give himself meaning. The question is whether the giving of thanks is not implicit in the ontological structure of our authentic being as men, and therefore whether our conquering intervention in the world in order to raise mankind (and here one could ask to what level?) is really the last word that can be said about man in the existential sense. Ethics are certainly necessary for the *human* cultivation of the world, but religion is not—even though religion is bound, via ethics, to give a distinctive complexion to this task and to give it the eschatological, definitive meaning which transcends, in grace, both all secularity and all ethics and which alone gives the world complete possession of itself.

Is religion unnecessary, then, to the secular plan, an "extra" whose meaning is to be found in itself, irrespective of its repercussions on the world? But, put in this way, is a religion which simply runs parallel to the created world still *real*?

All this presents us with a multitude of questions, but, to put it briefly, is Christianity concerned with God or with man? The radical theologians have passed final judgment on this already—it is concerned with man, and talking about God is simply an out-of-date Christian way of understanding man. Even Thomas Aquinas, who summarized simply the traditional Christian feeling in this matter, does not make it any easier for us. In his consideration of worship, prayer and the liturgy, he stated explicitly that worship is not necessary because of God, but because of man himself.[9] Not God, but religious man requires it, although in relation to God. But does man in a secularized world still require it? In any case, we still end up with the world again, in which man reaches his culminating point as a giver of meaning. The ultimate question, then, is whether man can really be called a completely secular being or whether the openness of his being as a person is not of such a nature that he cannot have his destiny within himself, not even in the "we" of relationship with another, since this too belongs within the sphere of the human person and has in its turn an unfathomable openness which cannot be filled by the secular. Man, though he is not wholly "of the world" is in the world. That is why his religious practice cannot, on the one hand, be divorced from the reality of his secular activity; for our view of God would then not really be taking his being as God into account. God is, after all, the creator of this secular sphere, and he does not take back with his left hand what he has given to us with his right. A religion which is not at the same time secular, then, can hardly be called authentic—but, on the other hand, this does not determine what religion and worship *are*. Nevertheless we can readily take as our point of departure the statement that religion—Christianity—is a definite, qualified manner of being in the world. I will therefore, and particularly in view of this special chapter devoted to worship, proceed to analyze the inner implications of this statement.

Secular Life as Worship

Paul wrote to the Christians of Rome that they should present their lives "as a living sacrifice, holy and acceptable to God" and as "spiritual worship."[10] Their "lives"—Paul said their "bodies" in the Semitic sense of all that belongs to man, the human person with all its secular implications. As a "body" man is with others in the world. This totality, the "world," as Paul said, is the place of "spiritual worship." In the Bible, among many other things, the "world" also means man in the world as God's good creation, deprived of glory by his sinfulness, but reborn in Christ as a "new creature" who is no longer doomed and who lives in a world liberated from the enslaving spirits of the world, of all kinds, both old and new. Christian life in the world, being concerned with the world and practising human solidarity, must therefore be, for the Christian, *worship* of God, glorifying God's name. Paul's admonition at the same time suggests that there is also a way of being active in the world that is not worship: there is Christian secularity and non-Christian secularity. Paul does not, however, imply that the Christian attitude deprives the secular of its integrity. It shares, still "groaning," in the "new creation," which is the Christian himself.

The Epistle to the Hebrews reveals the foundation of this early Christian view of worship even more clearly. Jesus did not give his life in a liturgical solemnity—on the contrary, in an obviously secular conflict, colored though it was by religion, he remained faithful to God and to men and gave his life for his own in a secular combination of circumstances. Calvary was not a Church liturgy, but an hour of human life, which Jesus experienced as worship. In it, our redemption is to be found. We have not been redeemed by an act of pure worship, a liturgical service—our redemption was accomplished by an act which was part of Jesus' human life, situated in history and in the world. "For the one of whom these things are spoken [i.e., our Lord] belonged to another tribe, from which *no one has ever served at the altar*" (Heb. 7.13). It is possible to speak of a secular liturgy, since the author of the letter to the Hebrews applied to this self-sacrifice in the world the cultic categories of Jewish religion under the old law, thus endowing it with their sacred character. In this way the new concept of worship came into being—human life itself experienced as a liturgy or as worship of God. Cult thus acquired a new meaning in the New Testament—life in the world shared with one's fellow-men must itself be a "spiritual sacrifice." On the basis of Jesus' self-sacrifice, the Christian's life in this world can now become worship. In their life of faith in the world, the people of God are now wholly a "priestly people of God." All believers are now told "to be a holy priesthood, to offer spiritual sacrifices acceptable to God through Jesus Christ" (1 Pet. 2.5). Faith itself is a "sacrificial offering" (Phil. 2.17) and every act of love of one's fellow-man is "a sacrifice acceptable and pleasing to God" (Phil. 4.18). Doing good, mutual help and sharing with one another are now, in Christ, liturgy and worship (see Heb. 13.16).

The New Testament clearly lays stress on "secular worship." Because the dawn of the eschatological life came with Christ —"And I saw no temple in the city, for its temple is the Lord God the Almighty and the Lamb" (Apoc. 21.22)—the profane or secular can become the pure expression of mankind's peace with God, as was fully apparent in the human life of Jesus.

That is why, for about three centuries, the first generations of Christians were proud of the fact that they had no churches or altars—one of the reasons why the pagans called them "atheists" or godless people.[11] The pagan Celsus censured Christians: "Your eyes cannot bear temples, altars and images of God"[12]—for Christians, these were "idolatry."[13] But the early Christians said this of themselves as well. Towards the end of the second century, Minucius Felix wrote: "We have no temples and no altars."[14] An absence of "religion" was the astonishing thing which particularly struck the pagans with regard to Christianity.[15] This primitive Christian reaction against worship as something separate from ordinary life was related to the prophetic impulse in the Old Testament: "Do not trust in these deceptive words: 'This is the temple of the Lord, the temple of the Lord, the temple of the Lord'. . . . truly amend your ways and your doings, . . . truly execute justice one with another" (Jer. 7.4–5). On the other hand, it is notable that as soon as Christians began to take over the external forms of pagan worship, the reproach of "atheism," as applied to them, disappeared from the writings of antiquity.[16]

Christianity in its beginnings, owing to a one-sided eschatological orientation in which it was constantly anticipating the end of time, made no distinction between the secular and the "sacral." "Whether you eat or drink, or whatever you do, do all to the glory of God" (1 Cor. 10.31). This *secular worship* was, so to speak, the novelty of the New Testament, in which a criticism of the old Jewish sacrifices and of the Old Testament distinction between profane and sacral, clean and unclean, is clearly discernible. The attention of the early Christians was directed less towards the Church than towards the kingdom of God, in which the whole of the created world was included. This eschatological Christianity saw the Christ not simply as the "head of the Church," but more universally as the one who had received dominion over the whole world. In Christ, Christians were no longer subjected to a world dominated by the powers of evil, but had themselves become the masters of the world—everything belonged to them, because they belonged to Christ (1 Cor. 3.22–3). Redemption thus meant an exorcism, a de-deification and a de-demonization of the secular. Fate, the *moira* or *fatum* of the ancient world, had been overcome. This was the "new creation" that had been accomplished in Christ on the basis of his dying to and through the "old world." In Christ, *amen* could be said to the secular, which could now be experienced as worship, because, since Jesus, "all the fullness of God" had appeared on earth (Col. 1.19).

Christian commitment to the ordering of human society here and now and Christian opposition to all injustice that disrupts peace among men—these may, then, rightly appeal to Scripture for their authority. In the situation in which Christianity finds itself in the world today, this commitment must be experienced as that secular worship required by the biblical essence of Christianity—secular life itself must be a "spiritual worship." Christian faith is not a flight *from* the world into the Church's liturgy. It aims to enable the world to share in the coming of the kingdom of God, a kingdom of peace, righteousness and love. Faith affirms that human life in the world is ultimately meaningful and worth living, thanks to Jesus, the Christ. The Second Vatican Council repeatedly stated this Christian view—the eschatological expectation of Christianity does not limit the Christian task in this world, but rather completes it in the light of new motives.[17] Christianity does not imply any neglect of the secular task, but, on the contrary, gives Christians a more intensive stimulus to carry it out.[18] Their eschatological expectation urges Christians to work for a better world for all peoples.[19]

But then we are faced with this question: Does Christianity then merge into a more intensive commitment to one's fellow-man in the world, experienced as secular worship? Is Christianity intensified human solidarity? Or is it a song of praise, a *paneguris* (Heb. 12.22) or a "festal gathering," in which the source of this greater fraternity which is experienced is praised in thanksgiving? Or, expressed in a different way: Is this intensified human solidarity, on the basis of the fact that God's revelation also gives man a deeper understanding of himself,[20] conceivable and capable of being experienced without any explicit praise of God?

The Liturgical Worship of the Church

The integration of the profane and the sacral is therefore an *eschatological* reality. But the Christian is living in the interim, in the period of tension between the "already" and the "not yet"—Christ's kingdom is still developing in history. The Church is not yet the eschatological kingdom. This is still only on its way, and there is, precisely for this reason, still a factual difference between the "profane" or secular and the religious. The first Christian generations had to learn empirically that the *eschaton* had only just been set in motion. They had therefore to reinterpret earlier statements in the light of their later existential experiences. They underwent the painful experience of discovering that, although he who was in the Lord could not sin,[21] Christians, like non-Christians, did in fact sin and die. There was still an element of sinfulness in their secular activity among men. Secularity in itself was not yet "secular liturgy." It was only secular liturgy by virtue of the Christian's faith in Jesus, the Christ, who made all things new.

Although the early Christians had no temples and altars, they did celebrate a Church liturgy in close connection with their "secular worship." Initially, these two were closely interwoven in the love-meal or *agape,* in which the secular liturgy of the community at table—"everything for the glory of God"—merged with the celebration of the Eucharist, so that

it was difficult to say where the one liturgy ended and the
other commenced. In any case, the reality of this secular worship, in its Christian dimension in depth, was explicitly cele-
brated in praising and thanking God and in preaching, in-
struction and admonition; in other words, in a Church liturgy
in which everything had to take place in accordance with
the order of the Church.

As I have argued elsewhere and still maintain,[22] man's
personal relationship with God can never occur in a "pure
state," because it would then be an *empty* relationship without
explicit content and religious man would be in danger of pursuing nothingness. Our love of God therefore always has—
has indeed of its very nature—a basis in the world and in our
fellow-men which brings it into the sphere of our experience.[23]
This does not, however, in any way imply that explicit and
thematic religion, as brought to expression in silence with
God (interior prayer) or in the ecclesial community of believers (the liturgy of the Word and the Sacrament), is the
consequence of an outmoded "theist supernaturalism."[24] Anyone who concludes, on the basis of the idea that man's living
and personal relationship with God is of its nature rooted in
and nourished by his relationship with his fellow-men in the
world, that the Christian has *only* to devote himself consistently to the humanization of mankind by humanizing the
world, without making any mention of God, is in my opinion
causing a short-circuit fatal to Christianity—it could only be
avoided by a consistent humanist atheism. After all, anyone
who states explicitly and thematically that man's relationship
with God is *implicitly* contained in his relationship with the
world and his fellow-men has already reached the level of an
explicit profession of belief in God—for how, otherwise, should
he have any knowledge of this implication? But then one

must accept the consequences of this explicit knowledge if one is to continue to be honest with oneself. As soon as one becomes aware that the shared experience of community with God makes one's service to the world and mankind a worship of God—in other words, as soon as one accepts "secular worship" as Christian—one must do justice to the fullness of this reality (which is precisely a gift) and express this affirmation in praise and thanksgiving.[25] Anyone who really gives and receives love in the day-to-day course of his life is conscious at times of a need to express himself in a gesture whose only significance is that it is a sign of his love and gratitude.

In the final analysis, "not expressed" or "never expressed" is the same thing as "irrelevant." But if we insist that God is the *implicit* happiness of our lives (and hence must remain implicit—that is, contained *in* our commitment to the world and our fellow-men), we are saying something without really wanting to express it. Humanist atheism seems to me to be a more consistent attitude. Moreover, experience teaches that this position of exclusive acknowledgment of God as the "transcendent third" in our human relationships cannot be maintained for very long—it soon turns either into explicit religion or the consistency of "atheism." In this respect, Paul van Buren's development is revealing. In a discussion about his book *The Secular Meaning of the Gospel,* he remarked frankly that he did not know what one gained or lost by calling a certain answer Christian or non-Christian. It seemed to him that one must say that around the figure of Christ Christianity has developed a fixed image of man and human relationships. So likewise has Western humanism. Whether and how far that humanism has been influenced by Christianity is a different question. If he were really pressed, he would probably say that he was more concerned with the content of that Christian image than with the name it was given, but if anyone wanted to make an issue of the name, he would have to admit that he was not quite a Christian.[26] His position is thus the direct opposite of that of the Christian Rudolf Bultmann. This does not, of course, mean that van Buren may not possess the *reality* of Christianity experientially. But it is legitimate to ask whether a grateful awareness of the event from which we may really be living is not decisive for the reality of such a life. And it is precisely here that the significance of the Church and her liturgy come into focus.

Anyone accepting "secular *worship*" cannot escape the inner consequence of praise and thanksgiving. That many can accept the former—secular worship—and in all honesty not the latter—praise and thanksgiving—raises the question of whether this is not the result of a one-sided tendency in Western civilization which at least for the time being is blinding men to the possibilities of anything in life which differs from the things which appeal to Western man today. In this case faith must be critical of this civilization—or at least, of its particular bias—and at the same time it must consider afresh the consequences of this new experience, that is, of the manifestation of God apart from explicitly religious or ecclesial forms. For if man's experience of the "hidden God" comes increasingly into prominence in our times, the manifestation of God in the liturgical event will be increasingly obscured, unless the presence of God in the form of genuine human solidarity is experienced in a more real way than in the past. Anyone wishing to make a case for both a Church liturgy and secular worship will therefore have to take this new Christian experience into account, since the faithful community must be brought to the recognition of itself in the liturgy.[27]

If then, praise and thanksgiving necessarily flow from the

fact that the gift has in reality been given, and hence are evoked in an inward way by "secular worship," the relationship between the Church's liturgy and secular worship will reflect this. The *berākhāh*—the praise of God from which the Eucharist first took its structure—or the Church's present liturgy will, of course, be without value if the reality which sustains it, our relationship of service to our fellow-men in the world, is not in fact there; for this secular worship in its deepest dimension, as the gift of grace, is what is expressed and acknowledged in prayer and the liturgy within the inter-subjective sphere of those who share the faith. Without secular worship, prayer and the Church's liturgy, our speaking of and to God become simply an ideological suprastructure without roots in the realities of life, and hence artificial. Our praise of God's majesty and of his love for men—"God is my song" —belongs essentially to the total structure of our love of God which realizes itself in love and concern for our fellow-men.

The rhythm, frequency and duration of this praise of God will naturally be determined by the prevailing social and historical conditions, and in sober and matter-of-fact times it will tend to be spread wider and thinner, although it is possible to argue that just such times are in greater need of warmth, splendor and elegance in the liturgical sphere. The Eastern liturgies are charged, somewhat unfairly, with "estrangement from the world"; yet it is remarkable how secular worship and Church liturgy are harmoniously united in some of these liturgies, as when they explicitly invite the faithful, at the beginning of the eucharistic service, to reconcile themselves with their fellow-men before joining in the sacrifice of praise. In the same way, Thomas Aquinas could say that "visiting widows and orphans" (the typically medieval form of social concern for one's fellow-men, which could be translated into

modern terms as help for the underdeveloped countries,
Christian protest against racial discrimination and all forms of
injustice) was itself worship, the glorifying of God's name,
but that this precisely called for an explicit praise of God and
Christian *eucharistia*.[28] It is already clear in the case of
Thomas, who derived this view from the very heart of
Christianity, that holiness and prayer are essentially identical
with concern for one's fellow-men in the world[29] and yet that
precisely this secular kind of prayer and holiness needs to be
expressed explicitly in praise and thanksgiving also. This is
expressed as *anamnēsis* in the eucharistic prayer, in which God
is praised and thanked for the miraculous deeds that he has
wrought in our humanity and its history.[30]

Without secular worship, the Christian Eucharist itself becomes meaningless for us. On the other hand, however, the
Eucharist is also the Church's *mission to* secular worship,
which has been made possible because of the absolute self-
sacrifice of Jesus' human life, suffering and death. Secular
worship and Church liturgy are not alternatives—they are
two complementary, mutually evocative forms of the one
Christianity. In John's gospel, the account of the washing of
the disciples' feet occupies more or less the same place as the
account of the Eucharist in the synoptics (the account that is
"lacking" in John). Many exegetes have therefore maintained
that the washing of the feet—service of one's fellow-men—has
a eucharistic significance. The Church's liturgy is a mission to
secular worship, to real service of one's fellow-men in the concretely existential situation of every individual and of the
whole of mankind in the world situation of the twentieth
century. The synoptics give an account of the *sacramentum*,
whereas John gives an account of the *res sacramenti*, the reality
that is signified and realized or to be realized—true fraternity

with all men, in Christ. To make a division between the Eucharist and world history (as worship) is to misconceive the deepest meaning both of the Eucharist and of world history, since the latter may move towards and merge into the *eschaton,* thanks to the *ephapax,* the unique event of Jesus' humanity— he who was in absolute community with the living God and thus the Son of God in secular humanity. Through the Church's liturgy, believing man is brought "to the core of reality," *in* the world *with* God. The world itself is now involved in the doctrine of "justification" which was, in the past, conceived in too intimate and individualistic terms both by Catholic and by Protestant Christians. In this sense, American theology will undoubtedly inject fresh life into its older and often pretentious European counterpart.

This totality is strikingly expressed in the term which became firmly established during the council—the Church is the *sacramentum mundi,* the "sign of the world," the world itself brought to epiphany. The Church and her liturgy are the world, with its secular worship, at that profound level on which the world utters its own *mystery* in a conscious and mature confession; that mystery from which and in which it lives, thanks to Christ, and thus fulfills and realizes itself precisely as Christ's world; in which man too gives thanks for his Christian life in the world which moves freely towards the eternal kingdom of God. Hence we *celebrate* in the Church what is being accomplished outside our churches in human history, insofar as this can be called salvation history. In the Christian unity of secular worship and Church liturgy, *homo mundanus* coincides with *homo religiosus.*

In this way, I believe, both authentic aspects—the one being present in what is called "secularized" Christianity and the other in what is known as "conventional" Christianity—are rescued from the silt of inauthentic expressions and forms which may have covered them both.

Is Church liturgy then simply communal thanksgiving and homage? Yes, it is, but in such a way that reality is intensified and the accomplishment of man's mode of existence in the sign of Christ's resurrection is enhanced in it. The liturgy, after all, is carried out in the Church which believes that God's promise is fulfilled in Christ. In the liturgy of the Church, this promise is therefore accomplished in us, in me, because I enact, together with the Church, the faith of the Church and thus come, in faith, into contact with Jesus Christ, on whom the Church places her hope. It is in the Church's liturgy that God's grace in Christ is made publicly apparent—the promise is made true *now* in me, in the celebrating community. It is in this witness of faith that the *public* confession of the Christian conviction is made manifest—the *sacramentum fidei,* in other words, God's saving act in our sacramental, liturgical, visible activity of faith. God's grace thus manifests itself in our terrestrial history in a way that is most strikingly transparent to faith in the Church's liturgy, as an integrating part of the whole to which our "secular worship" also belongs, that other worship in which the same grace manifests itself in a different way and thus makes itself felt in a different way.

On closer consideration, the basic intention of the modern "desacralization" of the liturgy does not make it so strikingly different from the liturgy of the first ten centuries as might first appear. In both cases, it is the ordinary "concrete things" of human life which represent and realize the holy. In the "cosmocentric" view of man prevalent in the past, attention was directed towards physical things in the great world of creation, so that naturally water, oil, incense, ikons and everything else that was materially visible were included as the expression of the Invisible. In the modern "anthropocentric" view of man, our attention is directed towards ethics—towards justice and love, and it is above all these realities of creation that are experienced as the manifestation of the Invisible.

In both cases, then, the point of departure is not an unjustified division between the world and the liturgy, but the insight in faith that the "new earth" is already being realized in a hidden manner. The believer who was orientated towards nature spoke above all of the "new earth." The present-day believer, on the other hand, prefers to speak of "new history," the "metropolis" and the "secular city" by virtue of the eschatological kingdom begun for us in Christ. The old exuberance of the "material signs" and thus of "nature" has given way to the new exuberance of human solidarity and thus of "history," but both express the *same* sacramental intention. Is this difference within the unity not a gain, a deepening and a humanization rather than a loss? In itself, it is in any case not a weakening of the sacramental experience, but a translation of this experience into a different social context —less orientated towards "nature" and more orientated towards "history," less cosmic and more emphatically human —and in both cases it is the secular manifestation or sacrament of grace.

Not only the physical but everything else which belongs to humanity is experienced as the sacramental manifestation of God's presence. It is precisely for this reason that the celebration of the community is once again stressed in the liturgy and that the communication of the divine is conceived *less* in material categories than in the "real presence" of Christ in his assembled people, who demand justice and love for all men. It is precisely for this reason that the present-day believer can no longer experience the real presence in the Eucharist "considered in isolation"—that is, experienced separately from Christ's real presence in the assembled congregation. It is not a question of denying one concept in favor of the other but of making the material world of *man in community* central, with the result that the *whole* becomes the sacrament of God's manifestation in Christ. The fact that the whole human person and his physical mode of existence are committed at the same time—a commitment in which the man Jesus has gone before us—prevents the liturgy from being one-sidedly either materialized or spiritualized. Human solidarity has therefore acquired its own sacramental form in the renewed liturgy, so that the breach between life and liturgy, a consequence of the change in the West from "cosmocentric" to "anthropocentric" thinking, in which the liturgy lagged behind, can once again be healed. Worship and life thus join hands more cordially, and the Church's liturgy is again becoming the *sacramentum mundi,* or rather, the sacrament of the *historia mundi,* of the world of men which, in the sign of Jesus' resurrection, moves towards the eschatological kingdom in which terrestrial history is, by God's power, perpetuated in eternity.

All this will have inescapable consequences for the further renewal of the liturgy, both in its content and in its structure. The liturgical cult will not be able to ignore the total structure of secular worship and its epiphany in the Church's liturgy. A liturgy which spoke only of the hereafter and ignored the concrete history of the world, which is precisely the place where the *eschaton* is mysteriously in the process of becoming, would be a liturgy which forgot the Johannine account of the washing of the disciples' feet, a *liturgia gloriae* which left out the period and the realm in which people are engaged with all their heart and soul. How could life and liturgy then form a unity, as the council asked, without making a division between the secular and the religious? If this division is not avoided, the Church's liturgy will not survive; it will become estranged from the world—and then Christians will, of course, abandon it.

If, on the other hand, the Church's liturgy were reduced to what presupposes and at the same time gives rise to liturgy— that is, "secular worship," in which God is only implicitly experienced in secular life, or brought down to the level of a pleasant little chat consisting of "good morning" and "have a nice weekend"—then this liturgy would be a serious misconception not only of the "spiritual sacrifice" implied by man's being in the world in the light of community with God but also of the profoundly human dimension which is expressed in the thankful celebration of all that gives our lives meaning and makes them worth living. And this is certainly no trivial commonplace, but the "seriousness of divine love," made historically tangible among us in Jesus' human love of God which had the form of a radical love of men "to the end."

As long as God is not "all in all," there is, it is true, no division between the Christian's life in the Church and his life in the world, but there is certainly an inner tension between them. The profane is not a category of the kingdom of God, because it is in the profane that the kingdom of God will completely penetrate the whole of creation and thus give it its highest autonomous freedom and its transparency to the divine. The profane is a provisional category—a category of the *coming* of the kingdom of God; of this kingdom's state of becoming. As long as this time of becoming lasts, so too will the duality of secular and Church worship remain valid and in force for the Christian. No practice of religion is possible which does not at the same time draw everyone and everything into its orbit, but without doing away with the secularity of the world. Secular activity is a part of the eucharistic sacrifice. Indeed, as for Jesus himself, so for the Christian, the "spiritual sacrifice" of everyday life in the world with one's fellow-men is *the* sacrifice that matters; it is in this life in the world that the Christian finds the *reality* of his living participation in the sacrifice of Christ, the sacramental form of which he may receive as nourishment in the Eucharist, as his confession in faith that secular worship is only possible by virtue of God's "new creation" in Christ. Thus the fact that the worship proper to human history in this world has become possible thanks to Jesus' absolute love of men, which was itself the worship of God, is presented to the whole world as a sign in the Church's liturgy. History is to be brought to a good end in Christ. This is the indestructible Christian hope which impels us not only to improve the world and militantly to resist everything that may make the history of salvation a history that is opposed to salvation, but also to praise and thank God in the Eucharist, a praise that will ultimately sound like the *berākhāh* which, according to John, Jesus pronounced on the eve of his death: "I glorified thee on earth, *by completing the work* which thou gavest me *to do*" (John 17.4). Glorifying God's name is building the world of men, by the power of Jesus, the Christ, into a "communion of saints," a kingdom of peace, justice and love, and at the same time "recollecting" that all this is an unmerited gift that is as characteristic of God—as "natural" to him—as is his entire being. This unquestioning divine goodness continues to be, for problematic human life, a problem which both attracts and repels and which is in any case unfathomable. The only adequate answer to it is unconditional surrender.

Notes

1. T. Altizer and W. Hamilton, *Radical Theology and the Death of God*, New York, Bobbs-Merrill (1966), p. 7. See also T. Altizer, *The Gospel of Christian Atheism*, Philadelphia, Westminster, (1966). p. 25.

2. Altizer and Hamilton, *op. cit.*, p. 5.

3. Ved Mehta, *Over God gesproken*, Utrecht (1967), p. 69.

4. *Ibid.*, p. 74. See also Altizer, *The Gospel of Christian Atheism:* "It is this passionate protest against the Christian God that is both strange and offensive to the common Christian, but to the radical Christian there is no way to true faith apart from an abolition or dissolution of God himself."

5. See P. L. Berger's sociological considerations in *The Noise of Solemn Assemblies*, New York, Doubleday (1961).

6. *Theology of Culture*, New York, Oxford (1964), p. 42.

7. Pastoral Constitution on the Church and the World, pt. 1, c. 4, n. 43.

8. G. Marcel, *Le déclin de la sagesse*, Paris (1954).

9. *Summa Theologiae*, II–II, q. 91, a. 1, ad 3; q. 89, a. 1, ad 2; q. 81, a. 1, ad 1, etc.

10. Rom. 12.1–2. See E. Käsemann, "Gottesdienst im Alltag der Welt," *Exegetische Versuche und Besinnungen II*, Göttingen (1965[2]), pp. 198–204.

11. See among others, B. Koep, "'Religio' und 'Ritus' als Problem des frühen Christentums," *Jahrbuch für Ant. und Christentum* 5 (1962), pp. 43–59.

12. Origen, *Contra Celsum*, VII, 62.

13. *Ibid.*, VII, 63–64.

14. *Octavius*, 32, 1: CSEL II, p. 45.

15. See also Justin, *Apologia*, I, 13, 1–2.

16. See E. Fascher, "Der Vorwurf der Gottlosigkeit in der Auseinandersetzung bei Juden, Griechen und Christen," *Abraham unser Vater* (Festschrift O. Michel), edited by O. Betz, Leiden and Cologne (1963), pp. 78–105; see also A. Harnack, *Der Vorwurf des Atheismus in den drei ersten Jahrhunderten* (Texte und Untersuchungen, 28, 47). Leipzig (1905).

17. Pastoral Constitution, pt. 1, n. 21.

18. *Ibid.*, n. 39.

19. *Ibid.*, n. 43.

20. *Ibid.*, n. 34, n. 36, n. 41 and n. 11 (final sentence).

21. "No one born of God commits sin; for God's nature abides in him, and he cannot sin because he is born of God" (1 John 3.9). *The Holy Bible, Revised Standard Version*, New York, Nelson, 1946, 1952. All scriptural quotations in this book are from this version, copyrighted 1946 and 1952 by

the Division of Christian Education of the National Council of Churches.

22. See "Het nieuwe mens- en Godsbeeld in conflict met het religieuze leven," *Tijdschrift voor Theologie* 7 (1967), pp. 1–27.

23. *Ibid.,* p. 12.

24. I have already defended this point of view in *Tijdschrift voor Theologie* 3 (1963), especially pp. 320 ff.; reprinted in *God en mens* (Theologische Peilingen 2), Bilthoven (1965), especially p. 144.

25. For *zikkārōn—anamnēsis* or thankful remembrance—in the Old Testament, see, among others, P. A. de Boer, *Gedenken und Gedächtnis in der Welt des Alten Testaments,* Stuttgart (1962); A. Weiser, *Glaube und Geschichte im Alten Testament und andere ausgewählte Schriften,* Göttingen (1961), pp. 280–89.

26. In a conversation between Ved Mehta and van Buren in Ved Mehta, *op. cit.,* p. 73.

27. See also H. Manders, "Desacralisering van de liturgie," *Theologie en Zielzorg* 62 (1966), p. 133.

28. See, for example, *Summa Theologiae* II–II, q. 81, a. 1, ad 1; a. 3; a. 4, ad 2; a. 8.

29. *Ibid.,* II–II, q. 81, a. 8.

30. *Ibid.,* II–II, q. 91, a. 1, ad 1 and ad 2.

IV

The Church as the Sacrament of Dialogue

"Dialogue produces miracles of discovery, opening to us the miracles of life."—Reuel L. Howe, *The Miracle of Dialogue*.[1]

In feudal times, when the patriarchal possession of great landed estates was normal in human society, the appearance of a Church with all the aspects of possessing in monologue a "great estate of truth" was, from the sociological point of view, more or less taken for granted. This characterizes, in very broad outline, the basic attitude of the Christian churches from the time of Constantine until roughly the Second World War and, as far as the Roman Catholic Church is concerned, until what is now known as her conciliar and post-conciliar period. The mentality and the structures of the churches were typified by an attitude of monologue.

I am, of course, well aware of the risk involved in putting the whole of the past under a single heading. There are so many historical facts which could easily contradict the sketch that I have just given of the Church's past. The prophetic element, based on dialogue, has never really been absent from the Church of Christ. The monologue of the "established" Church has again and again, throughout the whole of the Church's history, been contradicted by evangelical movements which have listened to the voice of the Spirit and seen the signs of the times. The dialogue that has taken place within these movements between the word of God and the contemporary situation, or the call to these Christians from the world and human society, has again and again resulted, for example, in the foundation of new religious orders and congregations which have hastened to the assistance of the Church and the world wherever human help was needed.

The new phenomenon which is taking place before our very eyes in our own times or is at least beginning to take place, is therefore not simply a new thing in the Church. What is new is that it is no longer a question of some individual Christian understanding the human and Christian art of listening ecclesially to the world of men and human society, and thus setting afoot a modest evangelical movement within the "established" Church as in the past. What is new is that the Church as a whole, including the Church as a hierarchy, has accepted dialogue with the world as a *principle* and as a *basic attitude*. This emerges clearly, in the case of the Roman Catholic Church, from the Second Vatican Council and from encyclicals such as *Pacem in terris, Ecclesiam suam* and *Populorum progressio*. In his encyclical *Ecclesiam suam,* Paul VI said: "For the inner impulse to love which strives to convert itself externally into a gift of love, we will use the now current term dialogue (colloquium)."[2]

The Church's Renewed Understanding of Herself and of the World as the Inner Demand for a Church in Dialogue

I shall not discuss here the secular factors which have led to a dialogue-type church, but shall simply indicate, against this assumed background, certain central elements in the repercussion within the Church of those human experiences which in fact have brought the Church to understand herself as a Church in dialogue.

At issue here are certain fundamental changes in emphasis in the Church's understanding of herself as it is to a certain extent officially formulated, on the basis of a new tendency in the Church, in the documents of the Second Vatican Council. These changes can be summarized as follows:

1. The earlier tendency to identify the Church too readily with the kingdom of God has been abandoned[3] and the idea of the Church as the people of God that is still on the way is more strongly emphasized.[4]

2. The erroneous or crude interpretation given in the past to the idea of "outside the Church no salvation" has been superseded.[5] It is thus becoming increasingly clear that salvation is not the exclusive possession of the Church.

3. The Roman Catholic Church recognizes the ecclesial character of non-Catholic Christian communities.[6]

4. She also recognizes the authentically religious aspects of non-Christian religions[7] and even the presence of the Christian "new man," and therefore of Christianity itself, in all men of good will.[8]

5. God's saving will is also more clearly recognized outside Israel and Christianity,[9] with the result that it cannot strictly be denied that there are elements of revelation outside Israel and Christianity.

6. Emphasis is laid on the Church as the people of God before any distinction is made among the various offices in the Church, and specifically before the distinction is made between clergy and laity.[10] It is the whole Church as people of God which has received the anointing of the Spirit and, in its general priesthood,[11] is itself the active bearer of the unique Good News and of Christian tradition.[12]

7. Finally, the Council has affirmed the saving presence of

God in the secular, political, social and economic. evolution of mankind.[13]

This summary, albeit incomplete, of the elements which have made the Church break out of her self-enclosure, concentrate less on herself and turn openly towards others clearly shows that there is a possibility of change from a Church of monologue to a Church of dialogue. These pronouncements by the Second Vatican Council at least acknowledge that there is witness to the truth outside the Church as well as in it, and that on this basis dialogue is necessary for the Church. To bear witness in monologue means failure to appreciate the truth that is present outside the Church.

But the mere enumeration of these factors might give a false picture of dialogue. It would be misleading to regard this as possible only because, and insofar as, the Church can recognize something of herself in others—in other words, insofar as she can interpret others as "implicit" Christians and thus, in the final analysis, not allow others to be *other,* but secure them in advance for Christianity by interpreting their outlook on life as Christian. That would make all dialogue impossible—because, for example, a Buddhist from his point of view can just as well regard a Christian of good will as an "implicit" Buddhist. This does not mean that I wish to deny the reality of what is called "anonymous" Christianity. But it is necessary, if dialogue is to be sincere, for others to be involved in that dialogue precisely as others and therefore precisely as non-Christians. This in no way denies the Christian conviction that in every dialogue Christ himself is, as R. Mehl has rightly stated, "le présent commun," who personally guides our conversation toward the full truth which he himself is.[14]

The remaining element for sincere dialogue, which is so far lacking, was formulated elsewhere in the council—namely, in the conciliar declaration of the freedom of religion and in the official recognition that, although truth is the characteristic value and norm of a consciousness whose activity is to know, it can only become a subjective and concrete norm as well if man is aware of this truth as truth. This is, in other words, the Church's recognition of the right of the human person to refuse to accept as truth, and to refuse to live his life by, anything which contradicts his own conviction of the truth.[15] Man can only live in human dignity according to his own inner conviction of what is good and true.

Both aspects then, the Church's new understanding of herself and her new understanding of the world, form the basis of the Church's change from monologue to dialogue. The whole of this fundamental change of emphasis can be summarized in the key-idea which inspired this change, even though it was not so used in any of the documents of the council. This is the idea of the Church as the *sacramentum mundi*.[16] *Mundus* ("world") in this context means the confraternity, or other-orientated existence, of men in the world—man's mode of existence in dialogue with his fellow-men. The Church must, according to the council, really be the sacrament of this brotherhood: "Ecclesia . . . signum evadit illius fraternitatis quae sincerum dialogum permittit atque roborat";[17] that is, the Church is "the sign of that fraternity which permits and strengthens sincere dialogue." As such the Church really fulfills the "ministry of communication" in the world. Wherever there are impediments to communication, the Church must lead the way in overcoming them. As Gibson Winter has said so succinctly, the Church has "the task of re-opening communication."[18] He went even further, saying that "the ministry of reconciliation of the servant Church is the restoration of communication to society."[19] The council's statement, "In Christ the Church is the sacrament—that is, the sign and instrument—of intimate *union* with God and of the *unity* of all mankind,"[20] is a confirmation of this in so many words. The Church is the sacrament of dialogue, of communication between men.

The Church's renewed understanding of herself and of the world makes it possible for her henceforth to enter into dialogue with everybody, without abandoning her "claim to exclusiveness," to use Karl Jaspers' term, which previously seemed to make sincere dialogue virtually impossible in advance both for the world and for the Church. What, after all, is the initial assumption underlying sincere dialogue? As Reuel Howe has correctly said, "The truth of each needs to be brought into relation with the truth of others in order that the full dimension of the truth each has may be made known. Such is the task of dialogue."[21] Assuming that this is the function and meaning of dialogue, then, we are at once confronted with the forbidding question as to how such dialogue can be conducted in all sincerity when one of the partners claims in advance to possess the full truth and to be always right. But such a view of the Church is not in accordance with the Church's true understanding of herself—whatever the form in which she has appeared in history may in fact have been. For, even though the Church of Christ may assert that the fullness of the Promises rests on her, as a service to the world, and that she has the task of guarding and preserving this and of making it historically true, she cannot assert that she is always right—history provides us with ample evidence to the contrary. The Church has a religious mission in the world and *thus,* in this mission, also a humanizing task. But for the task of humanizing the world as it is she receives from divine revelation no light other than that of all men and their experiences, and she has therefore to search tentatively for solutions. Furthermore, her *religious* claim, her "claim to exclusiveness" on the basis of Christ's promise, is made relative by the fact that she is still eschatologically orientated—still on the way, in history, towards the kingdom of God and not yet identical with the kingdom of God. It is only there, in the definitive kingdom of God, that dialogue will be unanimous praise, the unanimously uttered *Amen* to what has become visible in everything and is inexhaustibly self-evident, but which at present we can only call, in faith, the "mystery of God." The Church on the way is not yet the kingdom of God. She proclaims it,[22] and it is only in this way that she is permitted to anticipate, in a specific manner, the kingdom of God whose powers are already actively effective in her and in the world. She can only speak about what is still to come without having in fact *experienced* it, except in realizations which are still incomplete, limited and disrupted through belonging to the history of the world, and deprived of their glory by sin. Therefore, the Church can thematize or conceptualize what is still to come only to a certain extent. She does this in a proper but negative manner, and at the same time in a positive manner, but then improperly;[23] that is to say, never wholly adequately, and yet nevertheless really and authentically, the Church continually *reinterprets,* in groping fidelity, the unique message of salvation in every new sociocultural situation.

This implies that the Church cannot even fulfill her role and present her unique message to the world—the basis of her "claim to exclusiveness"—except in dialogue with the world and human society. Hence what initially seemed an insurmountable obstacle to genuine dialogue calls of its very nature, on closer inspection, for an attitude of dialogue—unless the Church listens to the world of men, her unique testimony will not get through in its authenticity in the world, and her proclamation will be unheard. Real dialogue—sincere and unfeigned—is necessary for the Church's unique witness, and this is not only because the Spirit is active outside the frontiers of the empirical Church and not only because the whole history of the world must be seen in the light of the ubiquitous, active presence of the living God, but in addition because it belongs to the inner essence of revelation to be the word of God *in* the word of man. The Church does not simply have something to *communicate*. In order to communicate, she must also *receive from* and *listen to* what comes to her from the world as "foreign prophecy," but in which she nonetheless recognizes the well-known voice of her Lord. The relationship between the Church and the world is thus no longer the relationship of a "teaching" Church to a "learning" world, but the interrelationship of dialogue in which both make a mutual contribution and listen sincerely to each other.[24]

Because revelation is in its inner essence the word of God addressed to men in history, the Church, which is, in serving the world, the serving subject of this revelation, is essentially a Church in dialogue. It is not in spite of, but because of, her fundamental "claim to exclusiveness" that the Church is bound to enter into dialogue with the world, and she *can* do this—not simply "go through the motions" of dialogue. In other words, dialogue is the proper and distinctive mode of existence for the unique witness of the pilgrim Church. Consequently, we can say that the world in a state of dialogue is giving the Church a real opportunity to bear witness in a unique way, and in so doing to *be* the "Church." The council expressed the idea in this way: "The Church does not deny how much she herself has received from the history and development of mankind."[25]

It even applies that principle to the manner in which the Church carries her unique message out into the world.[26] In a word, then, it is thanks to the dialogue with the world that the Church achieves her essential character as Church.

All that I have said so far about the Church's essentially dialogical character could, of course, despite the use of the modern jargon of dialogue, really be no more than an expression of a basic attitude of monologue. In his very carefully written analysis, *The Miracle of Dialogue,* Reuel Howe has justly observed that the churches must enter into dialogue, "not for the purpose of gaining, but for the purpose of giving,"[27] and Gibson Winter in *The New Creation as Metropolis* has further stated that "a democratic society desperately needs a Church which can participate in its public life without acting as a faction in search of private advantage."[28] Dialogue, then, considered as *method,* is ambivalent; it may be the expression of a genuinely dialogical Church, or it may only conceal the fact that a Church is still fundamentally monological. It is therefore not a question of dialogue as method; this may be simply the application of new tactics to the contemporary situation for the purpose of more efficient self-aggrandizement. At stake is the principle itself—the basic attitude of openness in dialogue towards the other as other, in which he is allowed to speak and is given a hearing and the opportunity to realize himself more completely in and through dialogue.

This principle applies all the more to the Church, which is certainly not present in the world for her own sake, but is there to give Christ's Good News of the kingdom of God which is to come. That is why the Church's dialogue must not be "self-centered"—it is rather a ministry or service of the Church, a *diākonia* or *ministerium.* Even more than this, the whole ministry of the Church, even the priestly office, belongs fundamentally to the category of dialogue, because the Church's ministry is, as I have said, the *sacrament* of mankind's dialogical mode of existence. The conciliar Pastoral Constitution expressed this idea in the following way: "The Church recognizes all that is good in modern social dynamism . . . The promotion of unity is most closely connected with the Church's mission, since she is in Christ as the sacrament, that is, the sign and instrument, of the intimate union with God and the unity of all mankind."[29] It is, moreover, an essential aspect of sincere dialogue that one is not thinking of oneself, but of the other, although a good dialogue will essentially enrich both partners and bring them to a clearer understanding of themselves. In the Church's dialogue with the world, both partners are tentatively seeking, even though their perspective is different.[30] In this dialogue, the Church is "omnium bono inserviens,"[31] serving the well-being of all.

I shall not go any further here into the question as to how far the Church has already carried into practice the principles and the program for dialogue with the world put forward by the council. The realization of this program in the Church as *Ecclesia semper purificanda*[32]—"the Church which always needs purification"—is clearly lagging behind the program itself. But the fact that the council did solemnly formulate the principle of sincere dialogue is in any case the beginning of a promising *metanoia*. And then, it is understandable that the Church should find this kind of change in her manner of functioning especially painful, and initially even disrupting, because it means that her earlier monological mentality and structures are subjected to both internal and external criticism, with the result that at the moment all her monological fortifications are undergoing violent assault. This is the inevitable consequence of the discovery of man's essentially dialogical mode of existence by the Church and the world.[33]

This change of attitude means that the Church, as she emerges from the past, has to undergo something of a conversion, to dissociate herself from the refusal of dialogue that is bound up with ideology and with out-of-date ideas and assumptions in the matter of faith. She has to turn away from the view of herself as a triumphant Church and turn to an understanding of herself as a servant Church able to confess that she is often searching, and never omniscient. This pain which the Church has to inflict on herself in the light of her renewed self-awareness, and which as a consequence of dialogue is also inflicted upon her both from within and from without, is, however, a salutary pain. It means that Christians must show not only understanding of and sympathy towards their fellow-believers and their pastors, but also boldness and courage. They must, however, be bold without succumbing to the spirit of energetic demolition, the new triumphalism of destructive "dialogue" which soon develops into a monologue "from below" replacing the earlier monologue "from above."

The Content of the Dialogue between the Church and the World

Before we discuss the content of this dialogue, a preliminary question must first be answered. Have we not all been too ready to assume that only two partners are involved? Can we separate the Church and the world so clearly and regard them as two partners who can enter into dialogue with each other?

In fact, the Church is built up of men in the world. As the council has said, "As formed of men, the Church is already present here on earth. She consists of members of the society of men on earth who are called to give to the family of the children of God in the history of mankind the form which must be further extended until the coming of the Lord. . . . Thus the Church . . . keeps pace with the whole of humanity and shares with it the same fortune in this world."[34] This means, however, that in Christians the "world" itself is present in the Church and that the dialogue between the Church and the world is, in the first place, an *inter-Christian* dialogue,[35] a dialogue among Christians themselves both about their unique testimony of the faith and about the promotion of the well-being of the world and society. For, though convinced of the one ultimate destiny of man, the Christian still accepts the "precise autonomy of the secular sphere in which he is active."[36] An inter-Christian dialogue between the Church and the world is thus possible. In this sense, there are various partners in the dialogue.

We can, however, go further. At present the whole of mankind does not belong concretely and actually to the sacramental *communio* of the Church, in any of the Christian denominations. The Church is more and more ceasing to be the "Church of the people (*Volkskirche*) and becoming a "diaspora" Church. In the accepted pluralism of modern society, she will gradually become more and more a Church to which people belong on the basis of personal choice and free decision (*Freiwilligkeitskirche*). Hence there are in the one human society large numbers of people entirely outside the Church's sphere and indeed that of religion itself who are working to build a more human world. The community of the Church thus encounters a community of people outside the Church who have different views of the same mankind and of human society but who are nonetheless active in the same worldly sphere as Christians. Here are other partners with whom dialogue is possible and necessary, not only with regard to the Church's witness and that of non-Christians but also with regard to this shared work of building up the world and promoting the well-being of all peoples.

Finally, we must also take into account another phenomenon which is generally acknowledged nowadays (and which is, moreover, connected with the theme that I have already discussed, that of the autonomy of the secular sphere and of the world which is present *in* the Church). This is that from the *sociological* point of view the Church is just one institution in society alongside many others, and like all other social groups, she is studied scientifically by sociologists. Sociologically speaking, the Church belongs to the common market of the world as one social group of people who are working, with or without other groups, to build up the world.[37] All these groups participate in the one task of working for the well-being of mankind. Because of their common sphere of work, dialogue is, from the sociological point of view, possible between all these different bodies engaged in working for the well-being of man, and what is more, because of social interrelationships, this dialogue is very necessary. In building up and extending the "secular city," all these groups have their own contribution to make, according to their differentiated and specialized functions. As a social group, the Church claims to have a special religious and ethical contribution to make to this work of promoting the well-being of all mankind. In view of the past history of the churches, the other groups (Christian and non-Christian) are, of course, still dubious about the distinctive contribution that the churches can make, because they still suspect the churches of engaging in this dialogue and this collaboration out of motives of self-interest, wishing to gain something for themselves. Nevertheless, it should be made clear to the world from all kinds of publications issued by the various churches, and as far as the Roman Catholic Church is concerned, from official documents such as *Gaudium et spes, Pacem in terris,* and *Populorum progressio,* that the churches are really sincere in their desire to advance into the world, meeting its needs in service, and that they regard this work of promoting the well-being of man not as a means of religious propaganda and of furthering their own ends, but simply as something done for the sake of the love that desires justice for all men. That is why the question is being put to the churches in various countries and by many different world movements working for man's well-being, What have you to say to us? What is your contribution to the great world-wide dialogue undertaken for the purpose of furthering the well-being of all peoples? That is why it is ultimately a question of dialogue between the life of faith within the Church (seen sociologically as one empirical sector alongside other sectors in the whole of society), and the secular, not directly religious, sectors of that same society (which are administered by Christians and non-Christians alike).

It is therefore clear that, although the Church and the world can neither be identified with each other nor entirely separated as two independent factors (the Church is not "the world," but neither is she "not of the world"), a real dialogue between the Church and the world in the sense we have been discussing is certainly both feasible and necessary. This, then, answers our preliminary question, and we can now go on to discuss the content of the dialogue between the Church and the world.

I have, of course, already spoken of the content of the conversation which directly concerns man's ultimate destiny—the Church cannot proclaim her unique message to historical men unless she does it in dialogue with this world and with those who have differently orientated ways of understanding man. But since this message concerns the whole man—including man engaged in his worldly task of making the earth a better place to live—the Church and the world are talking about the *same thing:* concrete man in the world and in society. But although they are talking about the same thing, they are doing it from different points of view. That is why dialogue is necessary and why both the world and the Church, owing to the special contribution which each makes, need a two-sided conversation about their work for the welfare of all men, a conversation in which, so far as worldly projects are concerned, the Church will be afforded the opportunity of becoming more the *Church* and of helping the world to become more itself and a better *world*. On both sides the partners in the dialogue, who will have to collaborate with each other, will be called upon to express the best in themselves. As G. Gusdorf has said, "to come into the world is to begin to speak," and "one must allow the best part of himself to speak."[38]

The sphere from which the Church has a special contribution to make to the dialogue with the world in view of building up the world and promoting man's well-being was very properly indicated by the council as follows: "thus the mission of the Church will show its religious, and by that very fact its supremely human, character."[39] In other words, the Church makes her contribution from the *religious* sphere. Using Paul Tillich's terminology, we could say that, whereas the world talks about man with his "direct concerns" in mind, the Church also talks about these "direct concerns," but in the light of her message with regard to the "ultimate concern" of human life.[40] As the council rightly said, "Since it has been entrusted to the Church to reveal the mystery of God, who is the ultimate goal of man, she opens up to man at the same time the meaning of his own existence, that is, the innermost truth about himself."[41] Her faith in the living God also leads man to a deeper understanding of himself, and that is why the Church's eschatological expectation in no way inhibits the building up of the world here and now, but fulfills it through new motives[42] and acts as a more intensive stimulus to the building up of the world and the promotion of the well-being of people,[43] because the *eschaton* also urges us to realize a better world on earth.[44] In Christ, history has, after all, become saving history.

The Church's actual contribution can, of course, vary considerably—it may take the form of encouragement and confirmation, help, collaboration or the taking of initiatives. It may also consist of criticism and protest. Her very faith in God's revelation and in the "better world" that is to come may cause the Church to protest against ideologies which underlie man's work for a better world on earth when she knows that these ideologies have an inadequate concept of man's deepest being. The Church is, after all, convinced that whenever man (or society) gives himself over, with "ultimate concern" and therefore in unconditional surrender, to objects which are not in fact capable of corresponding to his deepest desires, he will remain dissatisfied, unfulfilled and isolated, and the human person will suffer a loss of integrity.[45] Unconditional surrender is only meaningful if it is directed towards something that is itself unconditional and therefore touches us most deeply as men. P. Ricoeur has also pointed frequently to the fact that purely technical improvement and the whole process of the rationalization of culture, however necessary they may be, are on the level of the "instrumental," the level of the means and the subordinate meanings of human life. This process of rationalization has therefore been accompanied by a loss of meaning and by an obscuring of ultimate values—Ricoeur refers in this context to the "character of meaninglessness attached to a purely instrumental project."[46] That is precisely why the world is at present appealing to the churches as well for an answer to man's most fundamental problems: "As the modern world develops further, more and more men every day are asking the most fundamental question, or they are experiencing it at least as new and vital: What is man? What is the meaning of suffering, evil and death which still continue to be among us, however much progress is made? What is the purpose of these conquests which are gained at such a high cost?"[47] That is the standpoint from which the Church enters, in her conviction of faith, into dialogue with the world, with the well-being of people here on earth in mind.

But in this dialogue with the secular world regarding the ultimate meaning of human life the Church also commits herself to the "direct concerns" of this world, and in so doing she must allow herself to be guided by the autonomous laws of this world's structures and tasks.[48] A typical example is *Populorum progressio*. This raises problems in dialogue both for the people of God as a whole and for the hierarchical leaders of the Church. On the one hand it places a strong emphasis on the functions of the general priesthood of the whole people of God in the world, and on the other hand the function of the Church's hierarchy (always sustained by the whole community of the faithful) is given a different aspect. For in documents such as *Populorum progressio* and *Gaudium et spes,* although the Church's teaching office is indeed in the background, it is the pastoral and prophetic authority of the hierarchy that is especially stressed. In these documents the Church addresses her members with binding force "in matters which are subject to a continuous evolution";[49] she makes statements which are to a great extent based on non-theological information—that is, on the analysis of secular situations. Clearly the Church's ministry is emerging here in a new function, a role in which it is *critical* of society and at the same time socially *utopian*. This is plainly leading to a new self-definition on the part of the Church's teaching office, the prophetic (that is, critical and constructive) power of which is also dependent on continued *dialogue* with the world. The Church cannot fulfill this prophetic task with regard to the secular problems of man and society purely in the light of revelation: she must also listen to the "foreign prophecy" addressed to her from the secular situation, urging her to take decisions which will help to shape the future. These imperatives, or future-making decisions, cannot be deduced from revelation; they arise out of negative or "contrast" experiences which evoke the protest "No! It can't go on like this; we won't stand for it any longer!" Such negative experiences make us realize the absence of what things ought to be like. Thus "what should be here and now" is to a certain extent, though incipiently and still vaguely, already perceived. Protest is possible only where there is hope. A negative experience would not be a contrast-experience, nor could it excite protest, if it did not somehow contain an element of positive hope in the real possibility of a better future. The prophetic utterance issuing from contrast-experience is consequently protest, hope-filled promise and initiative which helps to shape the future. Out of such contrast-experiences have grown the protests against war, various forms of social injustice, racial discrimination, large landholding, colonialism, etc., and similarly the ethical imperatives prescribing what needs to be done here and now for the building up of more humane living conditions. The history of the future is being prepared and inaugurated through practical decisions or new ethical imperatives. The recognition of this fact is the peculiar feature of encyclicals such as *Pacem in terris* and *Populorum progressio*. In them a new self-understanding of ecclesiastical office comes into view, for in social and political issues the ecclesiastical authorities no longer seek merely to safeguard humanity's ethical past achievements; they seek rather to let the authoritative voice of the Church community be heard in the guidance of humanity towards a better, more humane world—which, for the faith and hope of Christians, can truly be called an ascent, in Christ, towards the definitive kingdom. The Pastoral Constitution has already formulated this principle: "To carry out such a task, the Church has always had the duty of scrutinizing the signs of the times and of interpreting them in the light of the Gospel."[50] Past experience makes it evident that this cannot refer to a theoretical interpretation, for then the decisions which should shape the future come, as a rule, too late. What is indicated is much more of a toe-to-toe contact with the world. Ethical imperatives have seldom been discovered by philosophers, theologians or the ecclesiastical magisterium. They arise spontaneously out of the concrete secular experiences of life; they impose themselves with the evidence of experience. Only afterwards are they given theoretical formulation, critical examination and foundation, theological and magisterial expression. All this demonstrates the necessity of the "pre-reflexive" dialogue of Christians engaged in the world. Otherwise, Christian love, however generous it may be, will fail to discern what needs doing here and now, and its efforts will inevitably prove deficient or come too late.

The conclusion of this terse and incomplete analysis is the following: what is called for is not only, nor even primarily, a reflexive dialogue, but rather the existential involvement of Christians in the world, a "présence au monde." This does not imply complicity with the world, but a saving Christian presence, the forerunner of that hope in a "new heaven and a new earth," a hope which *revolutionizes* our efforts for a better future on earth and one in which, at the same time, every socio-political order that already exists becomes of *relative* value inasmuch as it is not yet the new world of God's promise.

Since the whole of society is now struggling with the same problems which cut across all the Christian denominations, dialogue between the Church and the world also naturally means, both from the point of view of the Church and from that of the world, ecumenical conversations between the churches. The world itself is providing a new stimulus to ecumenical dialogue.

Finally, we must remember that the "world" in the Johannine sense of the word, the evil world, is not only a reality outside the Church—it enters the Church herself and plays havoc there. That is why every sincere dialogue—dialogue between the churches, the Church's dialogue with the world, and the world's dialogue with the Church—must begin with and remain based on *metanoia,* conversion, and (from the Church's point of view) the principle of *Ecclesia semper reformanda et purificanda*—"The Church will always need reform and purification."

Notes

1. Reuel L. Howe, *The Miracle of Dialogue*, New York, Seabury (1963), p. 11.
2. Encyclical *Ecclesiam suam*, n. 66.
3. *Lumen gentium*, n. 5.
4. *Ibid.*, n. 8, n. 9, n. 14, n. 21; *Unitatis reintegratio* (ecumenism), n. 2, n. 6;

Dei Verbum (revelation), n. 7; *Apostolicam actuositatem* (the lay apostolate), n. 4; *Gaudium et spes* (the pastoral constitution), n. 1, n. 40, n. 45; *Ad gentes* (decree on the missions), n. 2.

5. *Ad gentes*, n. 7; *Gaudium et spes*, n. 22, n. 57; *Lumen gentium*, n. 8, n. 16; *Nostra aetate* (declaration on non-Christian religions), n. 1; etc.

6. *Unitatis reintegratio*, n. 3, n. 19; *Lumen gentium*, n. 15; *Gaudium et spes*, n. 40; *Ad gentes*, n. 15.

7. *Nostra aetate*, n. 2, n. 4; *Lumen gentium*, n. 16.

8. *Gaudium et spes*, n. 22.

9. *Dei Verbum*, n. 3, n. 4; *Lumen gentium*, n. 2, n. 16; *Ad gentes*, n. 7; *Nostra aetate*, n. 1.

10. *Lumen gentium*, chap. 2 with regard to chap. 3.

11. *Ibid.*, n. 9, n. 10, n. 26, n. 34; *Apostolicam actuositatem*, n. 3; *Sacrosanctum concilium* (on the liturgy), n. 14; *Presbyteratus ordinis*, n. 2; *Ad gentes*, n. 15.

12. *Dei verbum*, n. 8, n. 10.

13. With regard to social developments for the well-being of all people, the Pastoral Constitution says: "Spiritus Dei . . . huic evolutioni adest"; see *Gaudium et spes*, n. 26.

14. R. Mehl, *La rencontre d'autrui* (Cahiers théologiques, 36), Neuchâtel and Paris, p. 57.

15. *Dignitatis humanae personae* (declaration on religion freedom).

16. See E. Schillebeeckx, *De Ecclesia ut sacramento mundi* (Congressus Internationalis de theologia Vaticani II, Romae, 26 Sept.–1 Oct. 1966), Rome (1967); K. Rahner, *Konziliäre Lehre der Kirche und künftige Wirklichkeit christlichen Lebens* (Schriften zur Theologie, pt. 6), Einsiedeln (1965), pp. 479–98. See also *Lumen gentium*, n. 1, n. 9, n. 48; *Gaudium et spes*, n. 45, n. 43.

17. *Gaudium et spes*, n. 92.

18. Gibson Winter, *The New Creation as Metropolis*, New York, Macmillan (1963), p. 130.

19. *Ibid.*, p. 103.

20. *Lumen gentium*, n. 1; *Gaudium et spes*, n. 42.

21. Howe, *op. cit.*, p. 121.

22. *Lumen gentium*, n. 5.

23. See E. Schillebeeckx, *Revelation and Theology* (Theological Soundings, I), part I, New York (1967), pp. 119–24; part II, New York (1968), pp. 98–105.

24. *Gaudium et spes*, n. 40.

25. *Ibid.*, n. 44 (per totum).

26. *Ibid.*, n. 58.

27. Howe, *op. cit.*, p. 97.

28. Winter, *op. cit.*, p. 145.

29. *Gaudium et spes*, n. 42; *Apostolicam actuositatem*, n. 14.

30. Encyclical *Pacem in terris*, n. 154; *Gaudium et spes*, n. 10, also n. 33, n. 46, n. 47, n. 91.

31. *Gaudium et spes*, n. 42.

32. *Lumen gentium*, n. 8.

33. "Reopening broken communication will inevitably tear and disrupt the internal life of the Church, but that inner suffering is the essential nature of the authentic presence of the New Mankind in the World"; G. Winter, *The New Creation*, p. 127.

34. *Gaudium et spes*, n. 40.

35. See also K. Rahner, "Vom Dialog in der Kirche," *Schriften zur Theologie VIII*, pp. 426–446.

36. *Gaudium et spes*, n. 36; *Apostolicam actuositatem*, n. 7, etc.

37. See, among others, D. Moberg, *The Church as a Social Institution*, New York (1962); J. Matthes, *Die Emigration der Kirche aus der Gesellschaft*, Hamburg (1964); J. Milton Yinger, *Sociology Looks at Religion*, New York (1963).

38. G. Gusdorf, *La parole*, Paris (1956²), p. 8 and p. 83.

39. ". . . ita ut Ecclesiae missio religiosam et ex hoc ipso summe humanam se exhibeat" (*Gaudium et spes*, n. 11, final sentence).

40. P. Tillich, *Biblical Religion and the Search for Ultimate Reality*, Chicago (1964), *Theology of Culture*, New York (1964), p. 7, *Die Verlorene Dimension*, Hamburg (1962).

41. *Gaudium et spes*, n. 41

42. *Ibid.*, n. 21.

43. *Ibid.*, n. 39.

44. *Ibid.*, n. 43, also n. 34, n. 36, n. 41.

45. P. Tillich, *Dynamics of Faith*, New York (Harper Torchbook), 1958.

46. P. Ricoeur, "Prévision économique et choix éthique," *Esprit* 34 (1966), 178–193, pp. 188–89.

47. *Gaudium et spes*, n. 10; the same idea is expressed by Paul Tillich in *Auf der Grenze*, Munich (1962), p. 114.

48. *Apostolicam actuositatem*, n. 7.

49. *Gaudium et spes*, n. 91.

50. *Ibid.*, n. 4.

V

*Church, Magisterium and Politics**

Recent actions and documents of high ecclesiastical authority, such as Paul VI's address to the United Nations, the encyclicals *Pacem in terris* and *Populorum progressio,* and for a large part also the *Pastoral Constitution on the Church in the Modern World,* have created a problem: What is the nature, the bearing and the obligatory character of such statements by the magisterium? For such statements are not directly based on the data of revelation but are also dependent on a good (or not so good) analysis of the actual situation of human society. Such statements by the magisterium are therefore also determined by nontheological information. And this raises certain issues for the theologian.[1]

I. TWO OBJECTIONS THAT WILL NOT HOLD

1. One cannot maintain that Pope or Council were not aware of the fact that these questions belong to the sphere of historical and contingent actualities. The Pastoral Constitution says explicitly that it appeals to the conscience of all "in matters

* This article, translated by Theodore Westow, is reprinted with permission. Concilium 36: FAITH AND THE WORLD OF POLITICS. (Glen Rock, N.J.: Paulist Press, 1968) pp. 19–39. © 1968 by Paulist Fathers, Inc. and Stichting Concilium.

that are subject to constant development."[2] The magisterium knows, therefore, that in this field it speaks more or less hypothetically, i.e., given that this is the situation of man and society.

2. The second objection is far more tenacious. Some feel that, although at long last Christianity has become nonpolitical in the sense of having rid itself of ecclesiastical politics and, although the world's own secular character has been recognized and confirmed as such by the Christian faith, Council and Pope are, in a roundabout way, again "dabbling in politics" and exceeding their competence.

I do not deny that the gradual and rightful recognition of the world's autonomy has led many Christians to a kind of "political liberalism," taking refuge in what is "spiritual": religion is a private matter, the world and politics belong to the world as such, while the Church's place is in man's heart, in one's private social ambiance, in the sacristy and the church of stone and bricks. Thus, Christians were not interested in politics and took part in it mostly in order to secure as many advantages for the Church as possible. On the other hand, this same "political liberalism" caused Christians to fight each other in political conflicts, convinced that in political matters Christians are wholly free, as if it does not matter whether political affairs are conducted according to the demands of the Christian message or not.

In its doctrinal section the Pastoral Constitution, which recognizes the world's autonomy, has nevertheless denounced the schizophrenic situation which separates *life in the world* from Christian life.[3] It stresses that the Christian message concerns man as a whole, also in his personal relationships, whether private or public, and in his labors to make this earth more habitable and worthy of man: "The Church's religious mission is by the same token a human one;"[4] "the Church is charged to show forth the mystery of God, man's last end; simultaneously she shows man the meaning of his existence, the intimate truth about himself."[5] Therefore, the eschatological expectation is not a brake on this building up of a human world but rather the fulfillment of it by adding new motives;[6] it is a more intensive stimulus toward this building up of the world and this promotion of all nations[7] because the *eschaton* stimulates us to bring about a better earthly future.[8] Therefore, the Church has "to serve the general welfare of all."[9]

Particularly the doctrinal part of the Constitution contains striking statements that are the more remarkable if we remember the history of what happened before its promulgation. It says that, although we cannot identify the humanization process of this world with the growth of the Kingdom of God, these two are very closely intertwined insofar as a better ordering of the human community contributes toward this Kingdom.[10] Several Council fathers protested against a radical separation between the future of this earth and the Christian expectation, and this led to a change in the original text. The *expensio modorum* (reasons for accepting an amendment) rightly explains that insofar as laboring for welfare on this earth is an aspect of concern for brother, an expression of charity, this commitment to a better future on this earth cannot be adequately distinguished from a commitment to the Kingdom of God.[11] Just as typical is the modification of the original text from: "The form of this world, distorted by sin, *will pass* away" to "*is passing* away." What was meant here is that in the world's progress toward a better future through concern for brother, the *eschaton* itself is already shaping history,[12] obviously not automatically, but through the commitment of love which demands justice for all, and, given the human condition, this is impossible without a concrete social and political order.

This shows that the very process by which Christendom is being extricated from an entanglement which tied ecclesiastical structures to political ones (caesaro-papism, all kinds of "theocracies" and the harnessing of the Church to particular régimes), has now made it possible for Christians to be involved through a genuine, Gospel-inspired commitment in the realities of the world of politics.

II. EVANGELICAL INSPIRATION AND
THE "SIGNS OF THE TIMES"

From what has been said it is clear that when the Church's magisterium speaks about social and political issues, it is founded on the specific mandate of the Church to proclaim and promote the salvation of the concrete human person. Therefore, the Church speaks out of her own historical responsibility for man.

It is precisely this claim that creates problems. It hardly needs demonstration that, just as all fundamentalism is abhorrent in the interpretation of the bible, so a biblical fundamentalism in political matters would have disastrous consequences. The Christian message does not provide us directly with any concrete program for political action. On the other hand, one cannot maintain that the choice of a particular social policy is an open question for Christians. Therefore, between the message of the Gospel and the concrete historical political decisions, some decisive element must intervene. This was clearly seen in the Pastoral Constitution: "To carry out this task the Church must *continually examine the signs of the times* and *interpret them in the light of the Gospel.*"[13] In other words, the Church cannot directly rely on revelation in these matters. Human experience and "nontheological" factors play a very important part here. Can we analyze the structure?

1. A General Structure

There is no need to insist here on the fact that if the Church cannot fulfill her mandate in this field except through dialogue with the world, this is by no means an exceptional case. It is not *in spite of* but precisely *because of* her claim to exclusiveness (*Ausschlieszlich-keitsanpruch*) that the Church *never* speaks exclusively from revelation, but is essentially a Church of dialogue, even in the witness to, and the proclamation of, the Good News. The actual situation, as the hermeneutical situation, is an essential element of the contemporary proclamation of the total evangelical message.[14]

I only recall this point in order to make clear beforehand that the contribution of nontheological information to the Church's magisterial pronouncements cannot be the immediate reason for the specific character of such ecclesiastical pronouncements about political matters. The same happens, for example, in a dogmatic definition where the Church tries to express the evangelical message in other than purely biblical words and concepts. The Church and the magisterium can never live *exclusively* on the "data of revelation." The relation of the Church to the world is not simply one of a "teaching Church" to a "listening world," but an exchange, a dialogue, where contributions are made from both sides and both sides listen to each other, even in the authoritative proclamation of the Church's unique message. There is no need to develop this further.[15]

In the case of a magisterial pronouncement on political matters, this dialogue character of the Church stands out because here directives are given for right conduct in *the field of the world as such* and not merely because the world is used to express truths of revelation in conceptual form, as is the case with doctrinal definitions. In this field of social and political action the Church takes up a position with regard to the world precisely as worldly. And this she does because of her function of service with regard to mankind's salvation. For example, she demands, or points to, agrarian reform. For this she can obviously not draw directly on revelation. Revelation does indeed impose on her a constant concern for brother. But this concern must be expressed in terms of concrete history. That this expression of concern demands here and now this particular measure and not another (for example, whether she should emphasize the right to property or rather the need for fair distribution and socialization), makes one wonder where the magisterium obtains this kind of knowledge, and on what the binding character of such of her directives would be based.

2. *The Particular Structure of Such Concrete Decisions*

1. I have already pointed out that it is impossible to derive any concrete political plan of action *directly* from the Gospel message. Some think that this is possible when we combine this message with a scientifically conducted analysis of our present society. On the other hand, one may say that even such a scientific analysis still leaves a wide choice of alternative measures, and does not imply that only this or that political measure is ethically binding here and now, whether for a region or for the whole world. Often a number of possibilities stand open which then usually give rise to different answers

according to different social tendencies, organizations or even political parties. And the fact is that the papal documents referred to and the Pastoral Constitution do not just leave room for various solutions but often refer to one particular concrete option. And here the problem becomes pressing: How can the Church justify an authoritative demand for specific options in political matters in such a way that, given the necessary conditions, it is no longer an open question for the Christian but requires him to act?[16]

Without denying the charismatic assistance of the Spirit in the teaching, sanctifying and pastoral function of the Church, but rather accepting it fully, I nevertheless cannot see in this charismatic assistance the immediate explanation of the final concrete choice made in such ecclesiastical pronouncements. For this might create the impression that we invoke the Spirit on those difficult points which we cannot explain and that we try to bridge the unbridgeable distance between general Christian principles and the many-faced concrete situation by appealing to an intervening impulse from on high which would decide the definite choice from among the many possible ones. The Spirit of God does not work as a stopgap, but in and through man himself. In this sense we may say that an appeal to the Spirit cannot *explain* anything, while on the other hand, we emphatically maintain as believers that we see the charismatic assistance of the Spirit become historically manifest precisely when we have analyzed the inner structure of such a concrete decision by the magisterium and have made it intelligible (*insofar as* free human decisions can be penetrated intelligibly). Thus, the factual analysis of this inner structure is also an homage to the Spirit.

2. Here we must discuss a general problem of ethics. Many start from a certain "duality" in ethical norms because they

proceed from an abstract and theoretical morality. Therefore, they talk of abstract norms that are generally valid and concrete norms that refer to a "precise situation." Thus, they draw the conclusion that general principles of ethics can never lead to a concrete situation by simple *deduction*. They are inevitably confronted with the question of how to bridge the gap between the abstract and generally valid norms and the increasingly complicated human social situation which can, as such, usually call forth a variety of possible human solutions and reactions. Moreover, while in some cases it may be of little importance what particular solution is found, there are many cases where only one particular answer is capable of promoting human dignity here and now and for that reason is truly morally binding.[17] If, therefore, on the one hand, the general principles cannot provide us with a concrete solution and, on the other, even a scientific analysis of the situation cannot give us an unambiguous and clear solution, it follows, in the opinion of those dualists (general norms *and* strictly situational norms), that there must be somewhere an unknown third factor to act as a catalyst and to release the one proper and obligatory option from among the many. This catalyst would then *either* be a "supernatural" one, the guiding power of the Spirit, which breaks through the ambivalence of the problem, *or* some human, irrational factor such as intuition, or an unrationalized sympathetic hunch, an imaginative sense of history, etc.

One may ask whether the starting point of such reasoning, the abstract norm *and* the concrete norm, is the right one for this problem. I do not deny the significance of abstract, generally valid norms in the total context of human life. The question is, however, whether we place them in the right context and see them in their proper function in such a way that they show at the same time that a mere situational ethics would provide no solution. I cannot fully deal with this here, and if I did, there would not be enough space left for the real problem, but some points have to be mentioned.

Abstract pronouncements cannot seize hold of the reality simply *by themselves;* if they nevertheless possess a realistic value, this can only be derived from our total experience of reality. For instance, "to be human" is not a part of the real, i.e., individual and concrete human person side by side with another part which would constitute the individuality; for the individuality determines "being human" from within. Only and exclusively as intrinsically individualized is "being human" a reality and can it be the source of moral norms (which in religious parlance, we can rightly describe as the will of God). Therefore, there is only one source of ethical norms, namely, the historical reality of the value of the inviolable human person with all its bodily and social implications. That is why we cannot attribute validity to abstract norms as such. Moreover, no abstract statement can produce a call or invitation. The abstract and general nature of the norms simply shows up man's inability to express the concrete reality exhaustively. These abstract concepts appear in fact only as an aspect of a more integral human awareness of experience in which they obtain, due to the concrete existential contact with reality, the value of an inner objective reference to this experienced reality: only in that direction, indicated by the abstract conceptual pronouncement, lies the concrete reality, and in no other. But for the rest, the abstract content cannot determine this direction in the concrete.

Therefore, these abstract, generally valid norms are an inadequate yet real *pointer* to the one real, concrete ethical norm, namely, this concrete human person living historically in this concrete society. Ethical norms are requirements made by reality, and the so-called abstract general norms are but the essentially inadequate expression of this. Therefore, it is not the inadequate expression which, by itself, constitutes the ethical norm, but it is a pointer to the one and only norm: these persons who must be approached in a love that demands justice for all. The abstract expression can only indicate in a vague and general way the content of this one, concretely determined reality as it calls on me; therefore, I can never see in an abstract norm what I must do or not do here and now. For the same reason, namely, because these general norms express, however inadequately, at least something real about the concrete reality, my concrete decision must never fall *outside* the direction indicated by these norms (if, of course, correctly formulated). These general norms are directives, derived from earlier experiences and indicating a moral appreciation of basic human values without which human life would simply become absurd. And thus we overcome a morality that is either purely abstract or mere situation ethics.

If, then, for all practical purposes, the problem is not one of a confrontation between general norms and strictly situational elements, but one of respect for, and the promotion of, the concrete human person in his concrete society, the question is still: How do we know, or how does the magisterium know, what should be done in practice within the present society in order to contribute as a Christian to an existence that is more in line with man's dignity for this particular part of mankind in this particular society? How does such a constructive ethical investigation proceed?

3. The Pastoral Constitution states that we must "examine the signs of the times and interpret them in the light of the Gospel"; that means, we must interpret the concrete reality of society as the expression of a moral demand made on the

Christian conscience. But human history shows that this is not primarily a matter of finding a theoretical interpretation of these "signs of the times," because when we do that, the prophetic voice of a new moral imperative is usually heard too late. Elsewhere the Pastoral Constitution (46) speaks more realistically about a concern with urgent problems "in the light of the Gospel and of human experience." The past has shown that, long before the Churches had analyzed the social problems, there were people who, in their commitment and in a preanalytic dialogue with the world, had already reached the moral decision that fundamental changes were required. New situational ethical imperatives have rarely or never been initiated by philosophers, theologians, Churches or ecclesiastical authorities. They emerge from a concrete experience of life and impose themselves with the clear evidence of experience. Theoretical reflection comes afterward, and so do the critical examination and rationalization, the philosophical or theological and official formulation. And so, after the event, such imperatives are put forth as "generally valid, abstract norms." All this brings out the essential need for a "living presence in the world." The Church cannot fulfill her prophetic task with regard to the worldly problems of man and society simply by appealing to revelation, but only by listening very carefully to that "foreign prophecy" (*Fremdprophetie*) which appeals to her from the situation of the world and in which she recognizes the familiar voice of her Lord.

When we listen to and analyze this voice of worldly prophecy, we discover that definite moral historical decisions and the initiation of new moral imperatives and directives are in fact not born from a confrontation between general principles and the result of a preferably scientific analysis of the social situation, but usually (though not necessarily exclusively) from those concrete experiences which may perhaps best be described as "contrast-experiences." The vocation, the concrete ethical decision of Cardijn (later Cardinal Cardijn) as to what he thought should be done here and now about some social problems, emerged, as he said himself, from such a "contrast-experience": his fellow workers' bitter resentment of the fact that he, a worker like themselves, was lucky enough to get the money to study. There are hundreds of such cases. The contrast-experiences of the two World Wars, the concentration camps, political torture, the color-bar, the developing countries, the hungry, the homeless, the underprivileged and the poor in countries where there is so much potential wealth, and so on—all these experiences make people suddenly say: "This should not and must not go on." And so develops the protest against war, social injustice, racial discrimination, the ownership of vast properties, etc.

In our present society moral imperatives and historical decisions spring, moreover, particularly from the experience of a collective evil, such as the too low income of certain sections of society, colonial exploitation, racial discrimination and other injustices. When we analyze these contrast-experiences insofar as they may lead to new ethical imperatives, we find that these negative experiences imply an awareness of values that is veiled, positive, though not yet articulate; that they stir the conscience which begins to protest. Here the absence of "what ought to be" is experienced initially, and this leads to a perhaps vague, yet real, perception of "what should be done here and now." This experience is of course but the preliminary stage leading to the proper reflection of both a scientific analysis of the situation and of a new assessment of principles gained from experiences in the past. Yet, without this initial experience, which evokes a prophetic protest, neither the sciences nor philosophy or theology would have been stirred into action. (Such experiences often lead even to new sciences such as the "polémological"—war-science—institutes and the sociology of religion.) Through these experiences man begins to realize that he is living at a level *below* that of his basic potential and that he is kept at this low level precisely by the pressure of existing social structures to which he is subject.

In the past, such contrast-experiences led conscientious people to the ethical imperative of charitable deeds in the private sphere of immediate interpersonal encounter (Vincent de Paul, Don Bosco, etc.). Today, in contrast with "medieval" man, we know that the social "establishment" is not a divine creation, but a cultural and man-made situation which can be dealt with and reformed.[18] Historical imperatives that now emerge from such contrast-experiences immediately tackle the reform of the existing society itself. In other words, this type of contrast-experiences now lead to the moral imperative of decisions in the social and political field. This shows once again that the new moral imperatives, based on negative experiences, are part of human history; the science of ethics then begins to reflect upon this and in the course of time a whole framework of generally valid principles (basic and detailed) is built up.

Therefore, it is not this ethical formulation which is either the most important or the most decisive. And this makes it still clearer that the concrete ethical decision is not a mere application of a generally valid abstract norm. For these contrast-experiences show that the moral imperative is first discovered in its immediate, concrete, *inner* meaning, before it can be made the object of a science and then reduced to a generally valid principle. For that reason there is no need for an appeal to a "third" factor which some want to introduce in order to bridge the gap between the "general norm" and the "strictly situational element." The initial creative decision which discovered the historical imperative directly in its *inner* meaning in the very contrast-experience *is,* for the believer, at the same time the charismatic element of this whole process. The general norms, on the contrary, are the mapping out of a long history of experience (full of contrast-experiences) in search of a society more worthy of man, and doing so precisely on the basis mainly of these negative experiences.

This should make it obvious that a Christian's life is not very much helped by the magisterium proposing merely "general principles" for social and political issues because in that case the Church lags by definition behind the historical situation since such principles are the tail end of a preceding history, while the history of the future must be prepared by historical decisions and moral imperatives. To have seen this constitutes the real contribution made by such encyclicals as *Pacem in terris* and *Populorum progressio.* They deal really with definite moral decisions (though obviously against a background of basic principles already gained from past experiences).

So far, I have tried to analyze the concrete origin of moral decisions. There remains the specific Christian aspect to be dealt with in all this. Does the experience of our human existence guarantee that we *can* make life more worthy of man in a meaningful way? Does this not founder on man himself? Moreover, if a better future is the norm, does this belief in a better future allow us to sacrifice human beings in the present in order to achieve this better world in the future? The Gospel can indeed bring some clarity to this.

The heart of the message of Jesus' death and resurrection unto eternity lies in the proclamation that, by virtue of the Christ event, it is indeed possible to build up humanity and that this is not a labor of Sisyphus. In biblical terms this possibility is maintained, over against all human despair, when we say that this is the grace of God's Kingdom being achieved in man's world; it is a Kingdom of justice, peace and love, a Kingdom where there will be no evil, nor mourning, nor crying, nor pain (2 Peter 3,13; Apoc. 21,4). Christian hope knows that this possibility is given to man as a grace, and so the Christian lives in the conscious faith that his faithful commitment to a better temporal order is not in vain, although he does not see how this temporal order which is not yet the promised Kingdom, can be the obscure beginning of the *eschaton*. The hope of this radically new and final Kingdom stimulates him never to rest satisfied with what has already been achieved in this world. Historically we can never say *this* is the promised future. The Gospel called the one who said that "anti-Christ."

I agree with Ricoeur, Metz and Paupert[19] that this evangelical message gives us no direct program of social and political action, but, on the other hand, is socially and politically relevant in an indirect way, namely, in a "utopian" sense. But how should we understand this? The Gospel message of Christian expectation offers the stimulating possibility constantly to overcome the limitations of any present "establishment." It contains a permanent criticism of the actual situation: secular institutions, social structures and their dominant mentality. It urges constant improvement, and above all, it brings the firm conviction that this building up of a more human world is genuinely possible. We should not be afraid of the word "utopia" here, as it refers to that angle from where we can criticize society. Moreover, it is an historical fact that most of the "rights of man" which are now accepted (at least in principle), were initially considered by all well-thinking people as unrealistic and utopian dreams of peculiar individuals. The pressure function of a "utopia" is indeed an historical factor: mankind believes in what is humanly impossible. Moreover, the future with which we are concerned is not a mere accumulation of vague wishful thinking but something that was promised in Jesus Christ and becomes real, through grace, in history, and so possible for man. In a political society, the Christian expectation and the Sermon on the Mount play the part of an effective "utopia" which will keep on exercising an ever-present pressure on all social and political matters.

When we allow this Christian factor to play in human experience, particularly in what I have called contrast-experiences whence the new moral imperatives spring forth, it becomes clear that the protest prompted by these negative experiences ("this cannot go on") is also the expression of the firm hope that things *can* be done differently, *must* improve and *will* get better through our commitment. The prophetic voice that rises from the contrast-experience is therefore protest, hope-inspiring promise and historical initiative. To put it still more accurately: what makes the protest and the historical decision possible is the actual presence of this hope, for, without it, the negative experience would not prompt the contrast-experience and the protest. Thus the negative experience itself shows the primacy of this hope for a better future.[20] Is the history of these contrast-experiences not the soil on which in fact the profoundly human and religious notions of salvation and disaster ("non-salvation" —*onheil*) could grow? Moreover it is only when people become *aware* of the fact that a better existence than the "established" one is possible and indeed seen as realizable that protest appears and the need for historical decisions is sensed. Was it not this awareness, for instance, which has created a pre-revolutionary situation throughout Latin America?[21]

Because of the continuity in man's consciousness, where pre-reflexive experience and reflexive analysis meet in a complex unity, we can roughly distinguish two phases in these contrast-experiences: first, that of the negative experience itself, where the "utopian" urge of the Gospel provokes the prophetic protest against man's curtailment of the possibilities of his own existence, and where the moral demand for changes and improvements develops, with the result that in a vague way some concrete moral pointers begin to stand out; secondly, the phase where the message of the Gospel matures through a combination of theology and the scientific analysis of a particular situation into a responsible and more concrete plan of social and political action. In this way the Gospel message becomes indirectly relevant in social and political matters.

I agree, therefore, with Prof. J. B. Metz that we can truly speak of two functions of the Church, one that criticizes society and one that applies the "utopian" view to society.[22] And this should be understood in the sense that it is its "utopian" view which is the standard of its criticism. This holds for the Christian Churches as such, and therefore for all the faithful and particularly for the ecclesiastical authorities who, through their service, are responsible in the Church for the world. That something of this sense of responsibility *begins* to find a clear expression in such documents as *Pacem in terris* and *Populorum progressio* shows the beginning of a new self-awareness in the magisterium. It no longer merely registers the historical past in general principles but means to give a lead in those moral decisions that are opening up the future. In this sense we may call the Church *sacramentum mundi,* or rather *sacramentum historiae,* since we now see the historical dimension of the world as implied in the primacy of the future. For this reason we can attribute to the Church an institutionalized "critical function" with regard to the temporal order, a function based on a divine charisma. This has its roots in the prophetic character of the Church and thus in her hope of that promised future which starts already modestly in the history of this world as salvation history, i.e., as the gradual redemption of history itself.

This Christian expectation itself creates history in and through the commitment of the believers. This new self-awareness of the magisterium is the more valuable today as our present society with its indispensable involvement in rational planning urgently demands *collective* decisions in social and political affairs. That is why non-Catholics, too, watch these ecclesiastical decisions: Church and world are more and more convinced that they need each other's contribution for the sake of the one, communal, overall welfare of all mankind. Perhaps this new self-awareness demands that this critical function be better organized while individual Christians themselves (nourished on this "utopian" and "critical" contribution) no longer withdraw from concrete social politics but join in with all men of goodwill (but this, too, is an historical decision that affects the concrete situation).

The New Testament criticism of emperor-worship, together with its confirmation of the real and proper authority of the emperor, is already a symptom of this "utopian" and "critical" function of the Church with regard to society, and provides an authentic biblical foundation. This critical function can only be exercised through a genuine "presence in the world," through experiences where God, so to speak, inserts the world and history between himself and us as the perceptible *expression* (or "translation") of his call on us here and now. They are also the *medium* in and through which the Christian is made explicitly aware of this call. Lastly, they are the *sphere* within which he must embody his response to that call in his life. Thus, the world and history explicitly teach the Christian the concrete content of this call from God with regard to what happens in society. There the Christian should be first of all the active *prophet,* not of what can be achieved by power politics, but of that Christian "utopia" which brings about the *totally new,* all that is radically worthy of man, through his concern for his brothers. This "utopia" is the permanent source of criticism of all structures of life on this earth, but attacks particularly the existing situation insofar as it pretends to be already the realization of the "Christian order." This is not to deny the importance of a policy which aims at whatever can be reached during a given period of time. But it *does* mean that precisely in this case the Church and the individual Christian must continue to exercise a critical function, and that therefore the element of prophetic "unrest" must be kept alive. Eschatological hope makes the commitment to the temporal order *radical* and by the same token declares any already existing temporal order to be only relative. Thus the Christian's social and political commitment, rooted in his care for mankind, is the hermeneutic of what in Revelation the Kingdom of God's promise implies. The Church's critical function is not that of an outsider, pursuing a parallel path, but rather that of one who is critically involved in the building of the world and the progress of the nations.

III. THE MORALLY BINDING FORCE OF THE CHURCH'S MAGISTERIUM IN SOCIAL AND POLITICAL MATTERS

The binding force of statements by the magisterium on political, economic and general cultural issues can only be understood in the light of what has been said so far in this article.

I presuppose here that we are dealing with statements where the magisterium pronounces directly on the doctrinal background of a moral historical decision in the field of politics. But we are concerned here with the theological value of the "historical decisions" contained in such documents, in other words, of the value of a non-doctrinal, somewhat "hypothetical" pronouncement by the Church's highest authority, Pope or Council. The words "somewhat hypothetical" refer to the fact that such texts also depend on nontheological information and speak of a contingent secular reality. This is the same as saying that such a pronouncement can only have value insofar as a condition is realized: "given this particular historical situation of society." The concrete indications are therefore not, by themselves, valid for all times, or even everywhere here and now, since the situation may be completely different in various places.[23] Given the pace of development in today's society, these official documents may, therefore, be soon out of date, so that to keep on appealing to such concrete historical indications might soon become reactionary in the future. This is implied in the very definition of an "historical decision." Therefore, apart from possible inadequacies with regard to the analysis of the situation and past principles, social and political encyclicals appear in relatively quick succession and there are striking differences in their moral indications. Therefore, the Pastoral Constitution states quite rightly that the signs of the times must be *continually* examined. Given the situation, however, this specific pronouncement will hold here and now for the ecclesiastical community.

Basically, and first of all, the obligation lies in a demand addressed to all Christians and arising from the situation itself, insofar as it is seen as inhuman and unchristian. This situation ought to stir the Christian conscience even before any official pronouncement. The Church's intervention merely confirms this. The specific character of such an intervention lies in the fact that this demand is formulated in a clear, precise, concrete and definite sense (e.g., in this situation the breaking up of vast landed properties by expropriation is morally necessary). Although in many cases the concrete demand is meant to be understood as "illustrative" and leaves room for other possibilities,[24] occasionally such an official document puts forth a decisive choice in a way that rules out other measures. And history has often shown *after the event* that among various possible measures only one proved to be objectively right. Thus, we are faced once again and in a still more pregnant fashion with the question: Does the magisterium provide us, believers, with a guarantee that its specific indication is the only right one among many others? It seems to me that this can never be maintained in an *absolute* sense because concrete decisions in the field of politics can never have that kind of guarantee, not even when they proceed from ecclesiastical authority. We believe nevertheless that, functioning in and borne by the whole community of the Church, it stands under the charismatic guidance of the Spirit. We may say that this gives the Christian a moral certainty (within the limits of the "hypothetical" element referred to above) that whoever acts accordingly will really act more in line with what the situation demands, and that the Christian can therefore face the consequences of such an action more confidently, even if it should lead to complications. All this, indeed, is not so much directly concerned with obedience to the Church's teaching authority as with obedience to her pastoral prophetic function. This function does not have the same precision but a more powerful prophetic ability to "call forth," to stimulate a continuous search, and no Christian can close his ears, his heart and his inventive imagination to that. This leads us to the specific nature of the obligatory quality of these official directives. Because the concrete moral imperative grows mainly out of contrast-experiences, it has a primarily and principally *negative* character: "this cannot go on." What, for instance, peace may positively mean when we reject cold or hot wars, nobody knows. The Christian only has the vision of the "eschatological peace" (which he can only describe negatively for a large part). But in the experience of the concrete "non-peace" both our will to overcome this situation and the inventiveness of our informed love—seeking means to achieve justice for all—will grow apace.

And so this, perhaps somewhat abstract, yet significant analysis (so it seems to me) leads us to the conclusion that the obligatory character of a magisterial pronouncement on political and social issues lies rather in the "negative" aspect (this *must* change) than in something positive. The specific obligation contained in this positive element *shares* in the absolutely obligatory character of the negative experience, but to a degree which the situation here and now will determine. The "negative theology" in speculative matters shows us here the way to a "negative theology" in practical matters, in which the eschatological vision of the future is the positive, "utopian" and "critical" norm for this particular concrete and changing situation. A Christian, therefore, who has read, e.g., *Populorum progressio,* without any noticeable change in his day-to-day life, is guilty with regard to the prophetic voice of this papal document. He is guilty particularly with regard to mankind and God because he obviously accepts the existing order which the Bible qualifies as disorder. All social structures will remain subject to the criticism of the biblical message for as long as history lasts.

Notes

1. This problem was studied by K. Rahner, "Réflections sur la problématique théologique d'une Constitution Pastorale," in *Gaudium et spes, l'Eglise dans le monde de ce temps,* Paris (1967), pp. 13–41. I do not intend to repeat what he has said but rather to approach the issue from another angle without implying any criticism of Rahner. It is rather a *complementary* view.

2. N. 91. Also, *Pacem in terris,* n. 154.

3. N. 43. Tillich says in the same sense: "The existence of religion as a special realm is the most conspicuous proof of man's fallen state," in *Theology of Culture* (New York, 1964), p. 42.

4. *Loc. cit.* n. 11.

5. N. 41.

6. N. 41.

7. N. 39 and Ch. 4 and 5 (Pt. 2).

8. N. 43, also 34, 36 and 41. Cf. E. Schillebeeckx, "Foi chrétienne et attente terrestre," in *Gaudium et spes* (cf. Note 1), pp. 117–58.

9. Pastoral Constitution, N. 42.

10. N. 39.

11. *Expensio modorum,* in cap. 3, pars I, p. 236.

12. Pastoral Constitution, N. 39 (with corresponding *Expensio modorum*).

13. N. 4.

14. I have tried to explain this in Chapters I and IV of this book.

15. The Council admitted this: "The Church does not ignore how much she has received from the history and development of humanity" (Pastoral Constitution, n. 44), and it applied this explicitly to the way in which she expounds her unique message (n. 58).

16. The immediate obligation lies with the ecclesial community as such, and therefore on "faithful at large," not all individual faithful. Not every *individual* faithful is, for instance, called upon to go to a developing country, nor need he be a theologian although there must be theology in the Church. I am taking this point for granted.

17. The question is not that there is something relative and imperfect in *all* human decisions, also those of Church authorities. This is the mark of the human condition. I am referring here to the problem that specific historical decisions, however imperfect, can carry a moral obligation.

18. See among others, H. Freyer, *Theorie des gegenwärtigen Zeitalters* (2nd ed., Stuttgart, 1963), who, in 1955, was one of the first to analyze the tractability of the world and of society.

19. P. Ricoeur, "Tâches de l'éducateur politique," in *Esprit* 33 (1965), n. 340, pp. 78–93, esp. 88f.; J. M. Paupert, *Pour une politique évangélique* (Paris, 1965); J. B. Metz, "Nachwort," in *Der Dialog*, by R. Garaudy, K. Rahner, J. Metz (Reinbek, 1966), pp. 119–38.

20. I do not consider here the question how and how far it is possible, outside an explicitly Christian conviction, to have the firm will to construct a better world for all men, either as based on a positive reality which we, Christians, can *interpret* as an anonymously "Christian hope" (clarified through revelation), or as based on false ideologies, although this question is not without importance, also politically.

21. See C. Furtado, *La pré-révolution brésilienne* (Paris, 1964).

22. Cf. J. Moltmann, *Theologie der Hoffnung* (Munich, 1964); J. Metz, *loc. cit.*, and "The Church and the World" in *The Word in History*, St. Xavier Symposium (New York, 1966), pp. 69–85; P. Ricoeur, *loc. cit.* and "Le socius et le prochain," in *Histoire et Vérité* (Paris, 1955), pp. 99–111. Cf. also Chapter VI of this book.

23. See the qualification mentioned in n. 16. Moreover, the condition "given the generally described situation" remains always valid here. Because of the unification of the world and the consequently greater solidarity of people and of Christians, a given situation may well hold elsewhere though not in one's own country. The obligation is therefore influenced by all kinds of modifications.

24. This is why the Pastoral Constitution speaks of "searching out solutions of so many involved questions" (n. 46).

VI

The New Image of God,
Secularization and
Man's Future on Earth

In the past few months in the course of writing a series of interconnected articles,[1] I have been brought face to face with the unmistakable difficulties of contemporary Christians in a "secularized world." I wanted to look at the facts calmly, but while I was writing I felt an almost feverish sense of urgency because I was clearly dealing with a pressing problem which confronts all of us today, lay people and priests alike, at every turn. The passage of time has inevitably revealed certain inaccuracies in what I had written, but these seem to me to be of secondary importance in comparison with the basic conviction that has gradually been gaining ground in my mind—a basic idea which this series of articles seemed, on later reflection, to be no more than an attempt to express. The real, positive formulation of this idea that had been hauting me continued to elude me.

I feel that two experiences brought me to a new stage. On the one hand, I became directly acquainted with the "secularized world" of the United States and, at the personal level, with those who are called "death of God" theologians. On the other hand, I had a discussion, lasting a whole afternoon, with about forty French university chaplains. On the one hand, then, an encounter with what is usually known as "American pragmatism" and, on the other, an encounter with the typically anti-pragmatic *spiritualité* which is found in pastors who are active in university circles in France.

Both to the Americans and to the French I spoke on the subject of secularization and faith in God. In the questions that followed, I was brought into contact with two totally different worlds—the world of "efficiency" and the world of *spiritualité*. This was a challenge to me. It caused me to reflect again about the problem of secularization and faith in God and, in the course of this re-examination, I tried to assimilate the contents of a number of theological, and especially religious sociological, studies written by Americans which had previously been unknown to me. I now realize that it was this experience and this reading which brought me back to the basic idea that I had tried to formulate in the articles, but had only succeeded in half expressing or else had not put into words at all. I now believe that I have in principle arrived at a satisfactory formulation, although I have no grandiose illusions about what I am writing here.

I am aware that this introduction must sound pretentious, but after some hesitation I have decided not to omit it. It may help to demonstrate how theology cannot be simply a question of scholarship pursued within the walls of one's study, it can only be built up in dialogue with one's fellow-men, a dialogue which involves our whole lives, whether we shut ourselves off in anxiety or think together with others in hoping and seeking openness. What results from this is not something that can be regarded as a new system, and even less a sceptical "system of the nonsystem"; rather it is a simple reflection about that Christian faith and hope which is "always prepared," as a biblical tradition puts it, "to make a defence to anyone who calls us to account for the hope that is in us" (see 1 Pet. 3.15). Even for the theologian himself, theology today is a personal, living struggle. He must try to solve a real, living problem which no one can wave aside by triumphantly—or is it desperately?—brandishing uninterpreted conciliar texts. He has to settle a genuine living question which has risen to the surface everywhere, and he must do this without succumbing to current slogans or allowing himself to be driven into a corner by pressure from those who follow the latest fashion and automatically dub him either an out-of-date conservative or a rash progressive. Faithful to the gospel and its vital presence in the Church and open to the real problem of living people, the theologian must, without respect of persons, be able to say with Newman: "I am going my way."

This introduction, which is rather unusual for a theological article, will probably give the impression that I am anxious to safeguard myself against what follows. But it is really intended to claim the "freedom of the sons of God" for everyone who wishes faithfully to consider the evangelical message—to the sorrow or annoyance of those who, because of their conservative or their progressive attitude, are not open to genuine *metanoia,* not able to renew themselves and history in the power of the God who is to come: "renew yourselves, for the kingdom of God is at hand" (Matt. 3.2; 4.17). This, then is the real theme of this article.

The Danger of a New "Ideology"

It is impossible to avoid the impression that the "secularized world" is discussed today without nuances, as though it were a new and incontestable "dogma." Some sociologists and historians are therefore rightly beginning to question the very generalized use of this phrase and its content and meaning.[2] This has made me aware of the fact that a sociological concept and a theological concept of secularization are possibly being used interchangeably without any distinction.

If the phenomenon generally known as secularization is considered apart from all ideology, one is bound in the long run to conclude that this word refers to a very complex event, the basis of which is that man's relationship with the world and his social environment is radically changing. As I said elsewhere, this phenomenon is connected with religion only indirectly insofar as the image that we form of God and the way in which we experience religion are at work within the current image that we form of man and the world. There is a correlation between what we say about God and what we say about man. Religion, as a living, human reality in the world, is also a visible social factor and therefore implicated in all the great social changes that occur.

In modern society, science and technological planning are playing a more and more important part in the building up of the world and the promotion of the well-being of all peoples, and in this process man's earlier prescientific and pre-industrial attitude towards the world is radically changing. The two concepts of building up the world and promoting the well-being of all mankind are especially representative of historically *new* realities, since they have become possibilities only through the advances in science and the technological planning which has resulted. Formerly, man was orientated primarily towards the past, but now he looks resolutely towards the future. This revolution which has come about in man's attitude towards the world—instead of professing his belief in the primacy of the past (and thus of tradition), he is now actively engaged in claiming primacy for the future—may be called the exponent of the whole process of change.[3] Whether we like it or not, the ever increasing importance in modern life of the natural sciences, technology, and the behavioral sciences is thrusting man towards the future. Unlike the so-called humanities, which seek to reinterpret the past and thus to adapt it to present circumstances, these sciences are essentially directed towards the future and provide scientific and technological guidance for human society, which is clearly becoming orientated towards a new future.

Religion will always express itself and find its context in concrete human life and will always form a community that is incarnate in the world. Hence it is always a social factor. In former times it exercised its function within the society of the period, which was relatively stable, directed towards the past and intent on perpetuating the past. But the present radical change has obliged religion to function within a new society that is orientated towards the future. Man's religious experience today is therefore having to assimilate something entirely new —an industrial, urbanized world which, under the guidance of science and technological planning, is intent on creating a better future for mankind. This has, of course, meant that the churches have ceased to exercise many of the functions which they used to perform in temporal society. In the past, man and civilization had still not come of age from the scientific and technical point of view, and this meant a feeling of helplessness with regard to the things to be accomplished in the world; man's power had to be *supplemented* by religion. God, the hope of religious man, had in the past to function as his refuge in those secular spheres in which he had not yet achieved a firm hold on the world and human society. Looking back from our present position, we may say that God served, in those bygone days, as a substitute for the powers which man himself lacked. Now that man seems to be capable of coping with the world on his own, he no longer appeals to God and the Church to supply for his impotence. This aspect of the modern phenomenon can legitimately be called secularization.

It is, however, a fundamental ideological error to identify this function of God as a substitute—which was so closely connected with what was inherent in an earlier phase in man's social development—with the very essence of religion. This is no longer a sociological statement; it is a theological judgment, and what is more, a false judgment. The result of confusing these two concepts is that the whole change that is taking place today in our civilization, including its political and socio-economic aspects, is called simply "a process of secularization." This is an ideological error that cannot be justified even from the sociological point of view. Religious sociologists who have studied the whole phenomenon quite impartially therefore say only this—that the change that is taking place in society today shows *aspects* of secularization. To call the *entire* phenomenon secularization is not, they think, justified from the scientific point of view. In the first place it would involve taking a false concept of religion as the point of departure—and in what is, after all, a theological question. But in any case it is not possible to maintain that a view of this kind is based on an impartial scientific analysis of the facts—and facts are sacred in any authentic science. Naturally these sociologists do not deny that religion is involved in the whole process of change, but instead of referring to this phenomenon as "secularization" they describe it as a "radical religious change" of which secularization is only one aspect, a part of the total process which shows that religion is gradually dissociating itself from an older culture. But within the religious sphere this process of disengagement is accompanied by a simultaneous process of growing into the new culture which is coming into being. What is called the radical religious change is the product of this latter process.

In any event, it is unjustifiable from the sociological standpoint to apply the term which refers to one aspect or part of the total phenomenon—the loss of function of religion and the Church, which may correctly be called secularization—to the whole process. Through this error secularization is reduced to a pseudo-scientific concept which can easily be misused in the service of an ideology—if this generalized usage has not already been suggested by this ideology.

The consequences of this confusion are incalculable. Indeed it is possible to say that those who do call the total phenomenon "secularization" are drawing conclusions for the future with premature certainty: they state as their considered opinion that according to sociological analysis the world is irrevocably moving towards a future without God, and that in view of the unmistakably secularizing trend of history, religion and the Church can already be written off. But those who reason in this way are overlooking the fact that their point of departure is false—actually impartial sociological analysis has shown that only one aspect of the whole social revolution can legitimately be called secularization. A prediction about the direction in which history will move that is based on only one trend in a more comprehensive process of social development certainly will not find favor in the eyes of historians. Such predictions have been refuted again and again throughout history by the actual course of events. Moreover, this kind of unjustified claim is contradicted by sociological research itself, for it has already established the existence of various new forms of religious experience which are clearly not mere survivals from an earlier pattern of civilization—although it is, of course, possible to establish the existence of these elements as well—but which are obviously *different* forms assumed by man's present experience of religion in growing into a new cultural pattern. It is therefore impossible to avoid calling the generalized statement "We are living in a secularized world" a modern mythology.

If the total phenomenon is to be judged on the basis of one aspect, one part of the whole, then the new culture which is coming into being should by the same token be called a "deculturization"—certainly the presence of "deculturizing" elements can be established in what is taking new form today. The constraint of universal rationality under which the individual person and society are forced to live in an age subject to the rule of "scientific reason"—in other words, scientific omnipotence (which indeed seems to be proved from experience too!) —can quickly become unendurable, giving rise to uncertainty about this self-made world of ours. Owing to this uneasiness, "anti-system" movements are springing up everywhere. This is manifested in the social sphere by the emergence in large cities of "fringe communities" of all kinds, including the "hippies," who are characterized by their need for psychedelic means of extending the range of consciousness. In the religious sphere pentecostal movements and "underground" churches are being found increasingly attractive. The constraint imposed by rationality—the principle which is above all operative in the designing of a new society and a new future—is threatening to reduce man himself and the future to the level of things— mere material for objective analysis and planning. The younger generation especially is suffering under this pressure, which makes many young people seek refuge in an unreal world of so-called psychedelic experiences and impels many others to revolt and protest. It is a pressure which evokes all kinds of futuristic visions and poses more urgently than ever the question of the meaning and purpose of scientific rationality and technique. The question asked is no longer "What has happened to man?", but "What is going to happen to man?" This situation has resulted in scientists of different disciplines coming together for mutual consultation, because every science that is orientated towards the future has an inner necessity for seeking its own metaphysics and ethics.

The revolution that is taking place now in the direction of a self-made future therefore should not be equated with a glorified optimism about progress. We ought rather to say that human freedom is so heavily burdened by it that there is real danger, no longer of a flight from the world, but of a flight from the future, and in many different forms—the "world" has, in fact, become the "future."

In the Catholic Church, for example, the increasing phenomenon of priests leaving their office must, of course, be seen against the background of various factors present within the Church today. Nonetheless, I am of the opinion that this phenomenon must be viewed in relation to men's anxiety about the unstructured future—whereas in earlier times it was possible to say, simply in the light of the past, "This is the work of the priesthood and it is up to me to do it," henceforward the priest must discover for himself what his real work is. Everywhere the change in orientation from past to future is accompanied by a crisis of identity—this is natural. Like children entering adolescence, we are being forced out of the warm nest of our cultural past to set off towards a future which we must construct for ourselves.

But we should certainly avoid a generalized application of the term "secularization" just as carefully as we should avoid calling this total phenomenon "deculturalization."

*The New Culture as the Point of Departure
for a New Concept of God*

(1) From the sociological point of view, "secularization" therefore refers to only one purifying partial aspect of a radical change in man's experience of religion which takes place as soon as believers really want to take an active part in the present cultural transformation. It is permissible and correct to apply the statement "God is dead" fully to this one partial aspect, which is indeed secularization. But anyone who makes the mistake of applying the term secularization to the total development will likewise—and quite wrongly—understand the term "God is dead" in a universal sense. From the sociological standpoint he will have followed an unscientific course.

The objection can, of course, be raised here that sociology cannot provide an answer to the question of what is true. I should like to say first of all in reply that on precisely the basis of this sociologically unscientific designation of the whole process of social development as "secularization," the question of truth is already, in a considerable number of books and articles and in the spontaneous, unreflective conviction of many people, held to have been decided. Owing to this tendency to slip, quite unscientifically, from a sociological concept into a theological concept of secularization, the sociologically unjustified use of the term "total secularization" has been increased twofold. This has been the cause of immense confusion—the question of truth is regarded as solved by the sociologically analyzed facts! What has been forgotten in all this is, as Martin Marty has observed, that the statement "God is dead," conceived as an all-embracing utterance, is the clearest *non-secular* affirmation to be found among the secularists—it is as unverifiable empirically, and as metaphysical, as the statement "God exists."

And in any case, the sociologically analyzed facts also show us that there are still religious people, not only as a survival from an earlier civilization (in their factual experience of religion), but also as witnesses to a new experience of God.

In this chapter I do not intend to defend faith in God, on the basis of a new concept of God, apologetically against a secular interpretation of reality. I will simply take my own situation in the reality of the Christian faith as the point of departure and, on the basis of this, as a believer, clear up the problem of the cultural transformation in which believers are, of course, also involved. I will examine the possibilities of an experience of God that is really integrated into the new culture and of a new concept of God that really has its roots in this culture. Then I will investigate whether, on the basis of this, we can perhaps speak of the secularization of faith in an entirely new, theologically justified sense. Finally, I will put the question as to whether this new concept of God has anything to tell us about the existential anxiety with which man, in his self-made world, is obsessed and which impels him to treacherous flight from the future whenever he comes face to face with a future that he has to construct for himself.

(2) As far as man's experience of it and the forms in which it is expressed are concerned, religion is, of course, rooted in the culture in which it takes form. In our own period we are therefore seeing the emergence of a new concept of God which, as I have argued in earlier chapters, is nourished by the cultural soil of our historical situation, within whose structure the whole life of the believer is ordered. Hence the new concept of God is partly determined as to its explicit content and ideas by present-day culture—a culture not primarily directed towards the past but dynamically orientated towards the future. Philosophy, which is man's reflective sifting of the spirit

of the age, has therefore already begun to discuss the primacy of the future and a culture characterized by planning a better future for all mankind—the "principle of hope."[4]

Anyone who believes in God and is part of this culture will realize that his faith in God has lost its function as a substitute for human science. He will consequently begin to reflect again and to change his ideas of God. He knows that these are in part historically determined and therefore changeable, and he also knows in advance that even the new ideas that he is seeking will not remain valid for ever. But, on the other hand, he knows only too well that his idea of God cannot be relevant to his life if it is entirely at odds with the pattern of his own society and that new ideas of God that are rooted in his own culture will make faith something capable of being experienced by, and of appealing to, modern man, with the result that the Church's confession of God will gain in credibility in the world of today. I should therefore like to give an initial outline of the new concept of God which is now taking shape and in which the believer is trying to express an idea of the living God of "yesterday, today and tomorrow" that will be grasped and understood today. In doing this, I cannot, of course, go into all the implications of this concept of God.

In the older culture, orientated towards the past, whenever we thought or spoke of God's transcendence we used, almost automatically, to project God into the past. Eternity was rather like an unchangeable and petrified or eternalized "past"—"*in the beginning* was God." Men knew very well that God's eternity embraced man's present, past and future and that God was not only "the first," but also "the last" and therefore the presence whose eternal present transcended our present. The older theology had wonderful things to say about this, things which have in no way lost their value. But in that older civilization in which men's eyes were always turned towards the past, a powerful mutual attraction was felt between "transcendence" and eternity on the one hand and an eternalized "past" on the other. Now, however, in a culture which is resolutely turned towards the future as something that it means to make, what has in fact come about is that the flexible Christian concept of "transcendence," which is open to more than one meaning, is also affected by this shift. "Transcendence" thus tends to acquire a special affinity with what is called, in our temporality, "future." For, if divine transcendence really transcends and embraces, from within, man's past, present and future, the believer will choose, as soon as man has come to recognize the primacy of the future in temporality, to associate God's transcendence with the future, and he will be right in doing this. He will associate God with man's future, and since this individual person lives within a community of persons, he will eventually also associate God with the future of mankind as a whole. This, then, is the real seed ground for the new image of God in our new culture—provided, of course, that the reality of true faith in the invisible God who is the source of the movement impelling man to "form a concept" of God in the light of his worldly experience has been accepted.

In such a cultural framework, the God of those who believe in him will obviously reveal himself as the "One who is to come," the God who is *our* future. This, of course, brings about a radical change—the God whom we formerly, in the light of an earlier view of man and the world, called the "wholly Other" now manifests himself as the "wholly New," the One who is *our future,* who creates the future of mankind anew. He shows himself as the God who gives us in Jesus Christ the possibility of making the future—that is, of making everything new and transcending our sinful past and that of all men. The

new culture thus becomes the point of departure for the surprising rediscovery of the fact that the God of the promise
again gives us the task of setting out towards the promised
land, a land that we ourselves, trusting in the promise, must
reclaim and cultivate, as Israel did in the past.[5]

This "new," eschatological concept of God is already radically changing "theological treatises," and at an even deeper
level the whole of Christian life is also changing. In answer to
the contemporary question about the legitimacy of Christianity
and to the increasingly urgent question about the "verification
principle" of the Christian faith that is asked by the linguistic
analysts (and, faced with this question, a purely theoretical
theology often seems to be completely impotent), all that we
Christians can say, in the light of our faith in God as our future,
is that faith is not based on what is empirically and objectively
verifiable, but comes under the category of human existential
possibility. For this reason, the verification principle of the
Christian faith and its eschatological hope can only be stated
indirectly—it is to be found in the fact that Christians, as the
"community of those who hope," show in practice in their
lives that their hope is *capable* of changing the world now and
of making our history a real history of salvation which brings
well-being to all men, instead of a history without glory, opposed to salvation. A faith in God as the One who is to come,
as the future of the individual person and the community of
persons, must show its effectiveness in and to this world if it
is to avoid being dismissed as incredible because of the preunderstanding of our contemporaries. Faith which has as its
content the divine promise of an ultimate eschatological fulfillment for every man and in every moment of our lives proclaims God as the One who is to come—and, what is more,
as the One who is to come in the very history that he nonethe-

less transcends—has to make this believed promise come true in history and has to do this precisely by making this history *new*. Believers themselves will have to show, in their total commitment to life, where the richest springs are that can overcome the evil that deprives man of his joy and improve the world by really caring for man. In their total commitment, they will have to show who they are who have the power to protect the constantly threatened dignity of man and to bring salvation here and now. At this level, faith in God as the future for man and mankind will have to prove itself true.

Of course, this new concept of God implies a criticism of the earlier idea of God and of the concrete practice of Christian life that resulted from this idea of God. Anyone whose entire being is, culturally and religiously, orientated towards the past inevitably runs the risk of leaving the world as it is, of interpreting it, but not changing it—this was Karl Marx's legitimate criticism of the religion of his time. This attitude also runs the risk of by-passing the terrestrial future and taking hold of the post-terrestrial directly. In our new culture, however, Christian faith in a post-terrestrial future can only be seen to be true if this eschatological hope shows itself capable of bringing mankind a better future here and now. Who could believe in a God who will make everything new "later" if it is in no way apparent from the activity of those who hope in the One who is to come that he is already beginning to make everything new *now*—if in fact it is not apparent that this eschatological hope is able *now* to change the course of history for the better? Christian commitment to the world by concern for man will therefore be the exegesis or hermeneutics of the new concept of God, in which God is really shown to be the "wholly New One." It will have to be clear from the concrete practice of Christian life that God *de facto* manifests himself as the one whose power can bring about the new future. It is only from the vantage-point of this exegesis of the new concept of God in and through total Christian commitment to life that we shall, in the second place, be able to reconsider the past so as to interpret or reinterpret it. In so doing, we shall understand how the earlier Christian experience of God was, in an older civilization, justified, but is nonetheless subject to the criticism of the biblical "God of promise" whom we have been permitted to rediscover as a result of the cultural change of today. The *identity* of the new concept of God with the original Christian message will have to come indirectly to light in the activity of Christians themselves. If a reinterpretation of the Christian message produces an activity in which its identity with the gospel cannot be discovered, this interpretation cannot be a Christian interpretation. It will therefore be apparent that there is a special kind of *understanding* which is appropriate to statements about faith—such statements, after all, have nothing to do with ideology.[6] Hermeneutics consisting of the very practice of Christian life are therefore the *basis* for the concrete exegesis of ancient, biblical or magisterial texts. The distinctive contribution that eschatological hope can make to truly human progress in the world for the salvation of all men itself interprets the dogma of the "kingdom of God," in which "neither shall there be mourning nor crying nor pain any more" (Apoc. 21.4). "According to his promise we wait for new heavens and a new earth in which righteousness dwells" (2 Pet. 3.13). This goal of Christian hope seems to have a positive content. It is certainly positive in its suggestive power, but on closer inspection it is first and foremost a powerful "symbol that makes us think," a call to us to transcend what *we* have made—war, injustice, the absence of peace, the absence of love. We have, however, also been promised, in an example or prototype, that all this will pass away—the historical act of the man Jesus Christ and God's setting of his seal on this life by what we, in faith, call "resurrection." This reality is the most powerful religious symbol of what is truly possible as the future, the future which has *de facto* already commenced in Jesus as the Christ.

In the Bible, the expression "to *do* the truth" is used for the Christian attitude described. This gives emphasis to a concept of truth clearly different from the western idea of truth that was taken over from Hellenism, an idea which contains a fatal division because of the distinction that it makes, in spite of all the careful shades of meaning with which it is used, between theoretical and practical reason. It is certainly not necessary to accept all the implications of American pragmatism for one to be convinced of the truth of what I often heard at table in the United States—"The proof of the pudding is in the eating." One has, however, to be on one's guard against a short-circuit that often occurs here in Christian thought. Because God has promised us a future of salvation in grace *despite* our sinful history, it is easy for us to believe that this future in grace falls vertically into the terrestrial event, which would otherwise simply continue to take place as history without salvation. But eschatological hope implies faith that the Christian, by God's justification, is responsible for the terrestrial event itself becoming a history of salvation. In and through his attitude of faith, then, the Christian is already seeking to overcome all that is opposed to salvation in this world, to resist everything that has made and is still making our history a history without salvation and thus to make salvation triumph more and more. Just as our sinful freedom makes our human history into a history without salvation, so too will God transform this history without salvation into a saving event *in and through* our freedom into which we have been liberated in faith. The believer not only interprets history—he above all *changes* it. Anyone who disputes this is clearly forgetting that human freedom is the pivot of the historical event—via human freedom, grace is thus able to change history itself. This was the reason why I believed that it was possible to say that the credibility of the Christian promise must be *indirectly* apparent in the practice of Christian life. In our new culture, then, a theological treatise about God will be the culmination and completion of an exegesis which consists in the practice of Christian life. If this Christian practice is absent, the Christian faith will not be credible to modern man, who is sick of ideology, and is always ready to express the irrefutable reproach, "Words, words, words."

The new concept of God—that is, faith in the One who is to come, in the "wholly New One" who provides *us* here and now with the possibility of making human events into a history of salvation through an inward re-creation which makes us "new creatures" dead to sin, thus radically transforms our commitment to make a world more worthy of man, but at the same time it reduces to only relative value every result which has so far been achieved. The believer, who knows of the eschatological fulfillment promised to mankind and to man's history, will be unable to recognize in anything that has already been accomplished "a new heaven and a new earth." Unlike the Marxist, for example, he will not even venture to give a positive name to the ultimate fulfillment that is to come. The Christian leaves the future much more open than the Marxist: in his view, the Marxist tends to close the possibilities prematurely. For the Christian, it is an ideological misconception to call one concrete stage in the development of human history the ultimate point.

It is of course, possible to raise the following objection to what I have said—that it gives rise to a new identification which runs parallel with what has been objected to in the older experience of faith; in other words, an identification between faith in God and the new culture. In reply to this, I should like to say that no such identification has been made— all that I have done is to describe how faith must *function* in the new culture. My purpose in this has been to prevent anyone who is wholeheartedly taking part in the new culture from letting faith remain an attitude that cannot be realized, something that alienates him from the world because it forces him to live in two worlds, the world of science and technology, in which he carries out his secular task, and a world of fantasy which he has to enter in his faith. Objections such as the one expressed above give the impression that the questioner is of the opinion that the Christian faith must be made perfectly clear once and for all. I am unable to agree with this claim. I feel bound to say only this—that we, as Christians, can only expect to settle the problems of faith within our own society. Later generations will have to concern themselves with their own period, and we cannot anticipate their problems. It is not possible to provide a justification of the Christian faith that will be valid for all time, but it is possible to do so for the period in which we are living. The Christian authenticity of our present culture differs from that of other cultures, whether those which have become obsolete or those which may perhaps take form later on. Everyone must achieve Christian authenticity within the form of his own culture.

It is still possible to go further with the objection to my argument and, although agreeing that no new identification has been made, say that this "new" God, known as the "power of the future," is surely a new projection. The only reply that

I can make to this is that this same objection can be made to every religious faith and to every concept of God, whether it is new or old or still in the distant future. But this is not under discussion here. All that I am concerned with is to examine *how* the believer in God, for whom God is *not* a projection, can express his profession of faith in God in the new culture—this, at least, is what I have had in mind in writing this particular article. In the light of this newly thematized faith, a fruitful dialogue can once again be opened with atheism and secularism. If we believers do not reinterpret our concept of God, the dialogue will to a very great extent be *factually* concerned with the different *cultural* worlds that the partners inhabit. The inevitable consequence of this will be that the perspectives of both the believer and the unbeliever will be distorted at the very outset of the dialogue, since when the believer talks about religion, he will be understood by the unbelieving partner as talking about a (past) culture.

On the other hand one should not forget the biblical basis of this so-called new idea of God. The new culture was only the occasion for our rediscovery, especially in the Old Testament, of the living God as "our future." Neither should one overlook the fact that, according to the Bible, the foundation of the eschatalogical expectation is the certainty in faith of communion with God here and now. When the Bible posits the primacy of the future, it does not intend to deny man's present communication with the God of the Covenant. Prof. Th. Vriezen rightly remarks: "The future expectation is based on the certainty of faith in the present relationship with God."[7] The foundation of *hope* is *faith* in Yahweh who reveals himself as the living God of the community. The neglect of this biblical foundation is an unmistakable drawback in some of the recent "theologies of hope." This neglect fosters an unjustified identification of the promotion of the well-being of all people with the coming of the kingdom of God.

Moreover, for Christianity the foundation, norm and criterion of every future expectation is its relationship with the past, i.e. with Jesus of Nazareth and what has taken place in him. The Church of Christ is prophetic, but only on the basis of her faith that Jesus is the Christ. The Lord is prior to every Christian community, and for that reason the "saving past" of Jesus, as it is relived in the preaching of the Church, implies a criticism of the religious interpretations of contemporary Christianity. Even for Jesus himself the direct relationship with God, whom he calls his Father, is the basis of his conception of the coming kingdom of God (E. Käsemann). Without this attention to the present relationship with God and to Jesus' past, which the Spirit "brings to our remembrance," even the new idea of God appears to be in danger of becoming a new mythology.

On the basis of the new concept of God which, in keeping with the Old and New Testaments, involves the believer fully in the world in which human history is taking place here and now and in which our Christian freedom, liberated in faith, has to transform man's opposition to salvation into salvation, it is indeed possible to speak of a total secularization, but of a secularization in a theological sense, not in the pseudo-Christian sense which eliminates the reality of God—omits it or simply does not discuss it at all. It is a question of secularization in the *theological* sense—in other words, of an attitude which recognizes the presence of God in our human history and which can help to bring about a future of salvation for all men by concern for our fellow-men. It is an attitude in which we, recognizing God in the man Jesus, also recognize him in our fellow-men, who call us to the love which seeks justice for all men. Our faith in God will then become "secular"; in other words, it will assume the form of a love of man which is opposed to history without salvation and which strives to transform the concrete reality in which we are placed into a history of salvation for all men. God does not therefore disappear—on the contrary, he will begin to penetrate the whole of our life on this earth. He will, it is true, not be so tangible as he was in a religious attitude which reserved one half of life for purely secular activties and the other for religious practices (a form of schizophrenia which even in the past was never recognized by genuine Christians!) Rather, he will appear in the guise of a servant who is entirely at the disposal of his fellow-man. Apparently absent, he will thus, because of his all-penetrating immediacy, be more intimately close to us. Religious man sees himself confronted with the task of committing himself heart and soul to the future history of mankind in the light of his faith in the God who is to come. In this, we shall hasten his final coming which is really nothing but the other side of his coming in grace itself, since his coming always runs ahead of our efforts. That is the paradox of Christianity—we tread in the footsteps of the God who is to come to us from the future and, in so doing, it is still we who make history.

(3) What, then, is the relationship between this Christian activity that is directed towards the future and other terrestrial planning for a better world? What is, moreover, the real contribution that Christian faith in eschatological fulfillment can make to the terrestrial planning of society for the advantage of man as an individual person and as a community? This contribution cannot and should not be regarded as a new form of "substitution" with regard to the secular ordering of the world, as though religion were there to supplement or cut across the distinctively human projects for the future as a disturbing

factor coming from outside. To anyone suggesting such an intervening role on the part of God or religion, it would be right to say, "*That* God *is* dead."

But this does not mean that faith has no message *of its own* to bring to the secular sphere. On the contrary, it fulfills a function which I would describe as "critical negativity,"[8] by which term I mean to indicate a positive power which continues to exert constant pressure in order to bring about a better world, without humanity itself being sacrificed in the process. The positive content of what is "humanly desirable," to use P. Ricoeur's term, cannot be formulated, but mankind clearly has some negative knowledge of it. In the long run, situations which are unworthy of man give rise to explicit protest, not in the name of a concept of what would here and now have been worthy of man which is already positively defined, but in the name of human values still being sought, and revealed in a negative manner in the contrast-experience of situations unworthy of man.[9] The Christian has as little positive idea as the non-Christian of what is worthy of man, either ultimately or here and now. He too has to seek fumblingly and consider various alternatives, keeping in the back of his mind, as he searches, human values already realized in history.[10]

But the Christian is not simply seeking what is "humanly desirable," the unknown, what is completely worthy of man —he knows, in his eschatological faith, that the God of the promise has bound himself to the realization of this also in Christ, even though the Christian cannot formulate the content of this promise in a positive way. He knows that it has been promised to him and to the whole of mankind as gratuitous grace, a gift which faith has inwardly to *make its own* and which must therefore begin to become a reality in our human history. The Christian knows that he receives the future to make it—he does not simply receive it as a "present" that is given to him, but receives it to "make it" himself, to bring it about. On the one hand, eschatological hope is not a passive state of waiting for the future, but, on the other hand, neither is it self-redemption, as though the promised future could be realized by human achievement. It is perdition—the opposite to salvation—that is found in man himself. Through his free acts, it is established in the history which he himself brings about—man is himself the acting subject of the "sin of the world." It is therefore not only necessary to humanize the world—the very first demand is to redeem man himself. The building up and the improvement of the world stumbles again and again over man himself! The future that brings salvation —Pannenberg saw this, in any case, very clearly[11]—can only be a genuinely human future if it is *reconciliation* in grace. Precisely because the subject making history is sinful man, the realization of a better future cannot be human self-redemption or simply the result of scientific and technological planning. But, as I have said, Christian redemption is not just an inward, private event and the redemption of history must not be held over until the end of time! On the basis of his inward redemption, with the "new heart" that he is given, redeemed man will have to redeem our concrete history.

The Christian's eschatological faith is therefore a critical function whereby every "left-wing" political effort to give a positive and definitive name to what is worthy of man is condemned as ideology.[12] But, on the basis of this faith in ultimate fulfillment, negative criticism is also directed to "right-wing" political tendencies which give an absolute value to the "established order" and rationalize it as a pattern of temporal society that has been sanctioned by the "eternal" God. What is more—and this eliminates in advance a danger that might threaten the "new concept" of God—this critical function of eschatological hope implies a criticism of all "negative dialectics" whose critical negativity is sterile, however closely the views expressed correspond to the reality of man's disrupted state, and remains incapable of providing any positive contribution to the improvement of the condition of mankind as a whole. Finally, eschatological faith also implies a criticism of every attempt which, purely on the basis of scientific and technological planning, claims to be able to realize a perfect future for the whole of mankind.[13] It is obvious that we can no longer do without science and technology in world progress. Yet in themselves they can only reduce man to the status of a thing. Rational planning for the future does not make a man a good man, nor do science and technology bring that redemption which is the condition for the building up of a future that is really worthy of man. In opposition to everything which would diminish the possibilities of humanity, Christian faith in the *eschaton* continues to play a critically negative part and, with regard to the building up of a truly human future, the same eschatological hope still says that the humanly impossible is made really possible in Jesus the Christ. The message which Christianity brings to the secular world is this—humanity is possible! And, in the light of our *theological* concept of secularization, we can now add this—humanity is possible through the resources of man himself, but that means through the resources of redeemed man with his "new heart," which is a very different thing from a new heart scientifically transplanted, although this too must be included in the all-embracing activity which makes our history a history of the sacred possibilities of life.

The Christian inspiration in socio-economic and political life is therefore directed, by its "critical negativity," against every image of man whose lines are strictly drawn or which presents itself as a positive and total definition[14] and against the illusory expectation that science and technology are capable of solving the ultimate problems of man's existence. The contribution that this Christian inspiration with its critical negativity can make to the improvement of our dwelling-place here on earth by caring for man is therefore this—it can exert a strong pressure towards overcoming these limitations and towards raising this activity up to the highest human level— a level which cannot be defined, the maximum level which transcends all human expectations. The fact that this distinctively Christian contribution to the building up of a temporal society really worthy of man is critically negative— although it is based on a positive hope—may perhaps make it appear insignificant. But it should not be underestimated. The basic question, after all, is whether what is "humanly desirable" can—again and again—be so easily recognized *without* a critical function. And from where else would this come, if not from the faith that God is man's future? For all men—and Christians are no exception here—are, as such, only *seeking* what is worthy of man without being able to formulate positively what this is, and it is furthermore nowhere apparent from history—apart from God's promise—whether what is worthy of man is ultimately at all possible. In his search for what is worthy of humanity man is always coming up against the sinfulness of man, which cannot be removed from the world by science (although this does make an indirect contribution). But we have to go a stage further and affirm that faith in the *eschaton* exercises a critical function even with regard to all positive historical realization—urging us to transcend what has already been achieved and attain the maximum salvation for all men. This implies, then, that eschatological faith, in relation to the historical reality of this world, essentially and consistently includes criticism of society.

Christian party politicians[15] usually speak of a "*positive* Christian inspiration" with regard to the socio-economic and political ordering of temporal society. If what is meant by this is that the Christian faith exerts a positive pressure and insists that what is humanly impossible is indeed possible, then I can readily agree with it. If, on the other hand, it is to be understood in a different sense, then I am afraid that Christianity is thereby being narrowed down into a special kind of "ideology." It is, of course, true that anyone who is constantly seeking what is "humanly desirable" and is, in this search, subject to the pressure and the critical function of faith in the eschatological kingdom may not relinquish the human value that has already been achieved in the previous history of man. What has already been positively acknowledged as worthy of man may not be sacrificed and has to remain valid as an inspiration for the future. Defense of what has already been achieved may, however, act as a check on the search for the "humanly desirable" which has not yet been achieved and remains constantly threatened. By definition, what has already been achieved is, after all—as is borne out by the constant pressure of escatological hope—always below the level of the maximum that can be achieved. Pure defense of what has already been achieved, then, would seem to me to be the basis of those "right-wing" political tendencies which are met with in the case of so many Christians, whatever their denomination may be. But this seems to me to be an essentially un-Christian interpretation of the Christian faith, which is directed towards the God of our *future*. It is also a misunderstanding of theological secularization, the attitude which strives to permit the fullest accomplishment of God's design *within* our human history. The gospel does not present us directly with any socio-economic or political plan of action. All that it does is to call on us to commit ourselves radically to man and society and to criticize, in faith, society as it is.

It seems to me, then, to be *theologically* more desirable—and this is, moreover, an urgent task—for this criticism of society to be carried out by the Christian churches themselves, and preferably by the churches acting in ecumenical unity. At the technological and political level, Christians themselves ought, in the future, rather to join the ranks of all men of good will who are seeking what is worthy of man. There they can make their voices heard in criticism expressed in the light of faith. After all, there is no specifically Christian anthropology and no specifically Christian political or social doctrine on which a confessional party might base its activity. It also seems difficult to see how a political party could be formed on the basis of the prophetic "critical negativity" which the Christian faith exercises with regard to secular society. At the level of the concrete organization of temporal society, the distinctively Christian contribution is to be found, on the one hand, in a commitment to the building up of the world by a concern for man which is radical for the sake of eschatological faith and implemented by all available scientific and technical means and, on the other hand, in a criticism which is based on and inwardly flows from this same Christian hope, a criticism that is directed towards every positive design of man which is presented as the last word or which in any way diminishes man's being. Thus, Christian faith in the ultimate eschatological fulfillment which transcends all man's expectations—in other words, faith in "the One who is to come" as salvation both for the individual person and for the human community as a whole—will always be critical of every form of individualism or of collective totalitarianism. It will take a positive part in the building up of a better future, but it will nonetheless always keep this better future open to a constant transcendence of itself. That is the specifically Christian contribution to all men's search for a future that is more worthy of every individual man and of all men collectively. Only this function is specifically religious, while at the same time it still respects the distinctive autonomy of life in this world with its socioeconomic, political and cultural aspects. It also respects the "negative theology" of the "new concept" of God: "By faith Abraham obeyed when he was called to go out to a place which he was to receive as an inheritance; *and he went out, not knowing where he was to go*" (Heb. 11.8). This negative theology, which is directed towards eschatological fulfillment, performs a constant critical function with regard to everything which would diminish man's being. How it would be possible for this critical function of eschatological faith to be taken over by a principle within man himself which leaves his redemption in grace out of account, one which might arise from a social and cultural secularization in which the supplementary functions of religion are discontinued, I simply cannot see. For without the dynamism of Christian hope straining towards an absolute future we are left with an ideological design of man which limits what is "humanly desirable" in advance. The inevitable result is scepticism with regard to the potentialities of our human condition or acquiescence in a total openness in which all values, and the possibility of their ultimate fulfillment, are brought into question—a view in which justice can never be done, either now or in the future, to the individual person as such or to the human community as a whole.

After all that I have said so far, it is hardly necessary to

stress again that obviously Christians must commit themselves
to all concrete plans for the building up of the human community, stimulated by a continual search for the maximum of
human value that can be realized here and now. Their "critical
negativity" does not mean that they can simply stand by and
watch without working. Their critical function should not be
allowed to paralyze their positive efforts in the search for what
can and must be built up here and now provisionally, and
after all the circumstances have been considered—this would
be in complete contradiction to the radical Christian commitment to make our human history a history of salvation.
Indeed it is even beginning to dawn on Christians that the
critical function of their eschatological faith is capable of in-
spiring an ethical imperative which will lead to revolutionary
measures (critically judged in the light of faith). Rather
hesitantly, but in all seriousness, theology is engaged in working out a "theology of revolution." The renewal in Christian
faith is not without bearing on the fact that various countries
in South America are at this moment in the preliminary stages
of revolution, in contrast with the past, in which these nations'
practice of the faith was, unfortunately, partly the cause of the
perpetuation of unjust conditions.[16] Christianity itself is beginning to redress its own injustices. Nevertheless I am personally a little wary of the concept of a "theology of revolution"—it seems to be developing into a modern ideology. I am
more inclined to go along with those who do not propose constructing a theology of revolution but simply wish to investigate
the ethical implications of an active Christian participation in a
revolution which a past history offering no human salvation
has made inevitable. This seems to me an essentially different
thing from a theology of revolution. Unlike ethics, theology can
only be a reflection on God's redemption of man by grace,

and in Jesus this saving work was accomplished in a manner very different from the one envisioned by the first disciples, one of whom attacked Malchus with a sword. And even when a "theology" for it is lacking, a revolution can certainly count on the support of Christians so long as injustices exist which cannot be rectified by any other available means. Until the promised eschatological kingdom comes, it will always be difficult to change any actual situation in which man is denied the means of salvation without "dirtying our hands."

I would therefore integrate faith in the God who is to come and radical commitment to one's fellow-men with the function of "critical negativity," which is their direct consequence, briefly in the following way: the humanization of the world, but directed towards the *eschaton*.[17] This would seem, in a modern interpretation, to be the nucleus of the old problem of "nature and supernature."

Finally brief consideration must be given to the inspiration which Christian eschatological hope affords to man under the coercion of the new rationality, full of existential anxiety and fear of the future. Christian trust exerts its effects upon the distress which man experiences at the prospect of becoming, so to speak, pure matter, as he is degraded to the level of an object of technological planning for the future. At the same time it is important to give a little thought to the bearing of Christian eschatological expectation on man's freedom of choice—that freedom of choice owing to which he must bear the burden of constructing and extending the future for himself: his mind reels when he thinks of the incalculable consequences in which his self-made world may result. (This has become apparent in the mixture of joy and uneasiness with which the recent transplants of vital human organs have been regarded, or when men face the probability of a future in which living men will, to all intents and purposes, be bound to the computer.) Things like these call for a Christian spirituality for the future. The problem could, of course, fill a separate article, and I shall consequently limit myself to the following brief remarks.

In this world directed towards the future that man himself makes, the central point of the Christian tradition known as the mysticism of the "dark night of the soul" will become once more a new field of experience. The world of the future will, by virtue of its mastery of material circumstance, give man a greater freedom of movement and thus make his freedom a burden that is too heavy for him to bear alone. This will create a new and hitherto unknown area wherein he may find his security in the God who is to come, for trust in God. The Freudian and Marxist criticism of religion has rightly unmasked the "childlike consolation" which people look for in religion when they find themselves helpless before the world. This does not mean that, for those who love him, God is not a "spiritual consolation," but such a consolation is no longer a protection against the difficulties of human existence nor a refuge from the harshness of life. According to all appearances, it would seem as though a function of "substitution" has once again been attributed to God in a roundabout way.[18] This is, however, not so. An "evangelical consolation" of this kind falls outside the scope of criticism of religion. Today this is frequently overlooked in preaching, but in my opinion that is a mistake. Man, overburdened in his freedom and left alone even by his fellow-men to make free decisions, need not ultimately feel lonely—as John observes in a masterly statement in his gospel, given as a pure interpretation of Jesus' life (John 8.16), "I am not alone; the Father is always with me." The fact that this basic Christian spirituality has waned seems to me to be one of the reasons for the defeatism in the Church and her apostolate. "Theological secularization" has not yet found its distinctive spirituality. Within this sphere of trust, we can indeed take on what is impossible and, what is more, we are even encouraged to undertake it. Something of the French *spiritualité* can, in this task, keep our American and Dutch pragmatism in the right perspective.

What about the Church?

The life of the Church, with her sacramental liturgy and her proclamation of the Word, is necessary for the nourishment of eschatological hope, for the strengthening and celebration of this hope in the community of those who hope and for the taking of this message of hope out to the world, in the light of this constantly growing inner renewal towards the "new creation." In virtue of this, the community of the Church in the world will—in connection with man's commitment to the task of improving the world by means of science and technology—protest critically in faith against all forms of human society which fail to understand the dynamics of what is "humanly desirable" in any way whatever, either because of a "right-wing" or "left-wing" policy. In the life of the Church, Christians celebrate and praise the God of man's future, the God who has power to transform a history without salvation into a saving event, in and through faith, which proclaims the presence of the *redeeming* God in the world and in our history.

One implication of this is that our mission cannot be identified with help for the emergent countries. For the Christian, both the gospel and the material aid are, of course, an expression of Christian hope and faith in the ultimate eschatological fulfillment which in Christ must begin to take form here and now. But the Christian who provides help for the emergent countries without bringing the Christian message is simply transplanting the problems of the West into the "third world." And conversely, anyone who wishes to proclaim the Christian message without providing help for the developing countries is not only proclaiming a message which will not be believed— since, without commitment here and now to one's fellow-man, it becomes narrowed down to an ideology—but is also depriving this message of the eschatological stimulus to make true, here and now, by our building up of the world in faith, the paradox of the God who comes above all *in* our history. In this case, the Word is narrowed down and reduced to a matter of "language," to speaking, and we shall be guilty of a failure to appreciate that our faith in the living God must above all be expressed in and through the *act* which brings salvation. In this sphere, the distinction I have already made can also be applied—if social and cultural secularization is thought of as defining total reality, then a new mythology which makes the Church's mission indistinguishable from help for the underdeveloped countries is being preached; on the other hand, theological secularization—that is, a secularization in which God's existence is affirmed— is misapprehended if the Christian missionary commits himself to his task without providing material help. In this context it should be noted that while we busy ourselves with the demythologization of the past, a critical review of our contemporary slogans will not be out of place! Otherwise we shall give the impression—and not simply the impression—that we hold the barbaric view that our contemporary stage of development, with its contemporary outlook, is the ultimate eschatological stage itself and the sum total of the whole of history, all thought and all religious faith.

Within the new Christian concept of God, the pastoral office of the Church too is moving towards a renewed understanding of itself—this is, of course, natural. Sustained by the entire community of believers, the Church will undoubtedly continue, by her *teaching authority,* to guard with solicitous care the integrity of the eschatological message on which the seal was set in Jesus Christ. In her *pastoral* guidance, however, the Church will also let her voice of eschatological hope be heard prophetically—and therefore without respect of persons—in criticism of society. As only a beginning, but nonetheless unmistakably, this note has already been sounded, for example, in the papal encyclicals *Pacem in terris* and *Populorum progressio.* This is an encouraging indication of a new self-understanding on the part of the Church's *magisterium.* The *office* of the Church is aware of being situated in a world which is planning its future and which has brought the Church's faithful to the fresh discovery of the living God as the "wholly New One," the God who is to come, the God who makes all things new and the God of man's future, who imposes on Christians ethical decisions within human history and in the light of the eschatological future. Who, then, can suppose that we are moving irrevocably towards a history without God?

Notes

1. See, in addition to the lectures published in this book: "Het nieuwe mens- en Godsbeeld in conflict met het religieuze leven," *Tijdschrift voor Theologie* 7 (1967), pp. 1–27; "Foi chrétienne et attente terrestre," *Gaudium et spes, l'Eglise dans le monde de ce temps,* Paris (1967), pp. 117–158.

2. See, for example, David Martin, *Towards Eliminating the Concept of Secularization* (Penguin Survey), Baltimore (1965); J. Milton Yinger, *Soci-*

ology Looks at Religion, New York (1963); Martin E. Marty, *Varieties of Unbelief* (Anchor Paperback), New York (1966); E. Gellner, *Thought and Change,* Chicago–London (1964); E. Hoffer, *The Temper of Our Time,* New York (1967); W. Cantwell Smith, *The Meaning and End of Religion,* New York (1963) and London (1964); R. N. Bellah, "Religious Evolution," in W. Lessa and E. Z. Vogt, *Reader in Comparative Religion. An Anthropological Approach,* New York (1965), pp. 74 ff. See also Th. Luckmann, *The Invisible Religion. The Transformation of Symbols in Industrial Society,* New York (1967).

3. The following are a few of the works which are necessary if we are to understand how these changes in society have come and are still coming about and if we are to construct a theological study of the involvement of religion in these changes: C. Wright Mills, *The Sociological Imagination,* New York (1959); C. B. Macpherson, *The Political Theory of Possessive Individualism: Hobbes to Locke,* Oxford (1962); H. Marcuse, *One-Dimensional Man: Studies in the Ideology of Advanced Industrial Society,* Boston (1964); and, of course, *The New Sociology. Essays in Social Science and Social Theory* (in honor of C. W. Mills), edited by I. Horowitz, New York (1964). See also M. Frisch, *Homo Faber,* Frankfurt a. M. (1957) and H. Freyer, *Theorie des gegenwärtigen Zeitalters,* Stuttgart (1963; first edition, 1955).

4. E. Bloch, *Das Prinzip Hoffnung,* Berlin (1954), the first attempt—in the light of Marxism—to conceptualize this feature of our culture.

5. This trend is already discernible in many different theological works, although the theme in these is still, for the time being, worked out in very divergent ways. Among the best known of these works are: J. Moltmann, *Theologie der Hoffnung,* Munich (1965); G. Sauter, *Zukunft und Verheissung,* Zürich and Stuttgart (1965); J.-B. Metz, "Nachwort," in *Der Dialog* (R. Garaudy, K. Rahner and J.-B. Metz), Reinbek (1966), pp. 119–38; *ibid.,* "The Church and the World," in *The Word in History, St. Xavier Symposium,* New York (1966), pp. 69–85. According to the prospectus, there is to be an article by K. Rahner on "Zur Theologie der Hoffnung," in connection with the dialogue between Marxists and Christians, in the new journal, *Internationale Dialog Zeitschrift,* the first number of which is to be published in 1968. H. Fries has written a number of sympathetic, but critical marginal comments, "Spero ut intelligam. Bemerkungen zu einer Theologie der Hoffnung," in *Wahrheit und Verkündigung* (M. Schmaus zum 70. Geburtstag), Paderborn (1967), pp. 353–75. What is more, the whole of W. Pannenberg's work can be interpreted in this light. See especially "Der Gott der Hoffnung," *Grundfragen systematischer Theologie,* Göttingen (1967), pp. 387–98,

and his contributions to *Theology as History* (New Frontiers in Theology, III), New York, Evanston and London (1967). Harvey Cox, who, in *The Secular City*, showed a strong inclination to join the "death of God" theologians, has, in his latest book, clearly found his way towards a Christian "theology of hope." See *On Not Leaving It to the Snake*, New York (1967), and especially the first chapter, "The Death of God and the Future of Theology," pp. 3–13. See also *Diskussion über die Theologie der Hoffnung*, edited by W.-D. Marsch, Munich (1968).

6. It may be felt that a Modernist influence can be detected here, but this is not so. In the first place, I have insufficient knowledge of the Modernist movement to have experienced its influence directly. I do, however, know enough about it to be able to say that the "Modernists" were reacting against a view which regarded faith exclusively as a "believing to be true" and that they consequently emphasized the existential aspect of faith. For this reason, they were wary of a *theoretical* orthodoxy "viewed in itself" and regarded orthodox dogma more or less exclusively as a norm for the practical Christian attitude to life. I dissociate myself from this interpretation because it took into account only one aspect of faith and denied other aspects. The decree *Lamentabili* rightly dissociated itself from one clear tendency in Modernism, that is, that a dogma had, according to these thinkers, a purely pragmatic significance in orientating the activity of Christians. This is, however, obviously not the intention of my argument.

7. Th. Vriezen, *Hoofdlijnen der theologie van het Oude Testament,* Wageningen (1966[3]), p. 467.

8. I have borrowed this suggestive term with gratitude from T. W. Adorno, *Negative Dialektik,* Frankfurt a. M. (1966), without at the same time accepting his "system of the non-system" or other aspects of his argument. In a different perspective, the expression had already been indirectly suggested to me by P. Ricoeur, among others, and especially by his perspicacious article "Tâches de l'éducateur politique" in *Esprit* 33 (1965), no. 340, pp. 78–93.

9. I have described the meaning of these negative "contrast experiences" more fully in chapters 4 and 5.

10. What has already been realized is afterwards formulated, and we speak then of "universal ethical norms," which are thus in fact the result of a whole history full of contrast experiences, a history which nonetheless still continues to seek the maximum of human value.

11. W. Pannenberg, "Response to the Discussion," in *Theology as History* (New Frontiers in Theology, III), New York, Evanston and London (1967); see especially pp. 251–52.

12. The fiasco of this ideology has been clearly analyzed from the historical point of view by R. Aron, *Dimensions de la conscience historique,* Paris (1961). 13. This myth is analyzed in *Säkularisation und Utopie* (E. Forsthoff zum 65. Geburtstag) (Ebracher Studien), Stuttgart (1967). P. Ricoeur, in the article mentioned in note 8, has also provided, in brief, a similar criticism.

14. In the book mentioned in note 3 (One-Dimensional Man), H. Marcuse has shown by sociological analysis that there is a positive design of man (an image of man and the world), which is either conscious or unconscious, at the foundation of the organization of all temporal society and of its institutions, with the consequence that the *limitations* of all social forms and institutions also become intelligible on the basis of this historically determined understanding of the world and of man himself. The disclosure of the largely unconscious image of man which is at the basis of the concrete organization of temporal society (and which has therefore given this society its limitations) is a *conditio sine qua non* for the overcoming of the limitations of the "established order." Going further on the basis of these ideas, Macpherson has also analyzed, in the book mentioned in note 3 (*The Political Theory of Possessive Individualism*), the implicit "image of man" that underlies the liberal and democratic structure of European and North American society.

15. The part systems of, e.g., The Netherlands, Belgium, Italy or Germany, where there are separate confessional parties, form the immediate background of what follows.

16. The World Council of Churches has even placed the "theology of the revolution" on its agenda. There have been both Protestant and Catholic demands for such a theology and attempts have already been made to satisfy them. See especially Richard Shaull, among other things in "Le défi révolutionnaire lancé à l'Eglise et à la théologie," in *Christianisme social* 75 (1967), pp. 39–40 (the whole of the January–February number is devoted to this question). See also L. Dewart, *Christianity and Revolution,* New York (1963). The Catholic exegete J.-P. Audet also offers a number of views in *Bâtir la demeure humaine,* Montreal (1967).

17. The Pastoral Constitution on the Church and the World, *Gaudium et Spes,* warns us, on the one hand, against identifying man's improvement of the world and the coming of the kingdom of God, but, on the other hand, says nonetheless that man's building up of the world in faith by caring for his fellow-man and with the object of creating true brotherhood certainly has a mysterious, inward bond with the coming of the kingdom of God (no. 39).

18. In any case, it is still not an established fact, as far as I am concerned,

that God could not have fulfilled the function of "substitute." If the existence of a real interpersonal relationship between God and man and the fact that God's love of man is not a *relatio rationis,* but his very living essence itself and therefore a *relatio realis* in the transcendental and relational sense, are accepted in faith, then it need not be regarded as absurd for God to take absolute and surprising initiatives on behalf of those who really love him. If, however, the starting-point is taken that God really has a personal contact with man who loves him, it should not be difficult to see that the form that this will take in a world that is scientifically and technologically helpless will be different from the form that it will take in our present society, which has come of age from the scientific and technological point of view. Otherwise, the dialogue between God and man will not be taken seriously. In this connection, we have no need, of course, to think of the miraculous cancelling out of the natural laws! This became clear to me when I was in the United States and boarded a plane almost every day for a month. It is only by subjecting himself to its demands that the pilot can control matter (in this case, the aeroplane) and obtain the results he wants, simply by allowing the laws of nature to take their course. The aeroplane itself takes no account of the intentions of its maker or of the pilot—only the blind laws of matter apply here. Man is not a conjuror who imposes his will on these laws: it is the fact that man accepts his own impotence and his subjection to them which is at the basis of all his technical achievements. It seems to me, then, that this offers a perspective for the insight of faith which sees that God, leaving nature sovereign in its own sphere and equally leaving the history made by man simply what man makes of it, can nonetheless cause what he wishes to happen in nature and in history (as the pilot did with his aircraft), for the good of those who love him (see Rom. 8.28). It is, of course, possible that I am allowing myself to be carried away here by my Dominican training, which was based on the *sola gratia* and on the dictum that "everything is ultimately grace." But I believe that this is genuinely *Christian* wisdom, given to us by the living example of Jesus himself and simply echoed by us, in our Christian endeavor, in halting and broken language.